*Also by Yona Zeldis McDonough*

THE FOUR TEMPERAMENTS (A NOVEL)

THE BARBIE CHRONICLES: A LIVING DOLL TURNS FORTY

# all the available light

## A MARILYN MONROE READER

YONA ZELDIS MCDONOUGH

A TOUCHSTONE BOOK
PUBLISHED BY SIMON & SCHUSTER
NEW YORK    LONDON    TORONTO    SYDNEY

TOUCHSTONE
Rockefeller Center
1230 Avenue of the Americas
New York, NY 10020

TOUCHSTONE and colophon are registered trademarks
of Simon & Schuster, Inc.

For information about special discounts for bulk purchases,
please contact Simon & Schuster Special Sales:
1-800-456-6798 or business@simonandschuster.com

*Designed by Chris Welch*

Manufactured in the United States of America

10   9   8   7   6   5   4   3

Library of Congress Cataloging-in-Publication Data

All the available light : a Marilyn Monroe reader / [edited by] Yona Zeldis
McDonough.
    p.  cm.
"A Touchstone book"—P.
Includes bibliographical references.
1. Monroe, Marilyn, 1926–1962—Criticism and interpretation.
I. Title: Marilyn Monroe reader. II. McDonough, Yona Zeldis.
PN2287.M69 A55 2002
791.43'028'092—dc21                                    2002021039
ISBN 0-684-87392-3

# contents

# contents

# acknowledgments

$\mathcal{I}$ would like to thank Paul McDonough, Kenneth E. Silver, and Ed LaMance for the many insights and observations they shared with me regarding Monroe's life and films. The able crew at the Barney Karpfinger Agency—Olivia Blumer, Joe Gramm, and Laurie Marcus—also have my sincere thanks. I was helped immensely by the skillful editorial guidance of Marah Stets, and later, Allyson Edelhertz. My thanks to Ted Landry, my production editor. Additional thanks go to Eileen Adele Hale as well as to Laurie, Ethan, and Melissa

x    Winogrand for granting permission to use the cover photograph, and to Dawn Troy and Lissa Fessus of the Jeffrey Fraenkel Gallery in San Francisco for facilitating this use. Finally, I wish to thank all the writers represented in *All the Available Light* for their refreshing, provocative, and unique contributions to this volume.

## INTRODUCTION

*I*magine the following scenario if you can: A woman, now approaching eighty, is seated with her husband in the audience of the City Center of Music and Drama one evening in the late 1950s. They are waiting for the curtain to go up on a performance of the New York City Ballet. It must have been an electric moment. Here is a young and yet world-class ballet company whose founder and main choreographer— brilliant Russian-born George Balanchine—is in his prime. The theater itself, built in 1924 by the Ancient and Accepted Order of the Mystic Shrine, is wonderfully antic and absurd, with fanciful tiles in bright colors studding the outlandish surfaces of its architecture.

What were they going to see that night? *Allegro Brillante? Agon? Stars and Stripes? A Midsummer Night's Dream?* And who might have been dancing? Allegra Kent? Maria Tallchief? Melissa Hayden? It almost doesn't matter; it was sure to have been a spectacular night. But as the woman sat there, reading her program notes and chatting idly with her husband, she began to sense a kind of hum in the crowd, a certain energy that seemed to gather and swell, despite the fact that the curtain remained motionless and the lights had not yet begun to dim.

What could it be? She and her husband looked at each other, puzzled. Then they began to look around. There, in a balcony below, sat Marilyn Monroe and her then husband, Arthur Miller. The intensity of the excitement continued to grow as more and more people began first to whisper and then intone, "Marilyn, Marilyn." Sporadic clapping began; quickly it turned into an ovation, with people on their feet shouting out her name. One can only imagine how the dancers must have felt as they pawed the ground with their pointe shoes, as they always do before a performance, and did a few nervous relevés backstage. The giddy applause, the wild, joyful adulation rightfully belonged to them on that night: who could have stolen it? I'm sure that at some point they learned the answer and had to go on with the performance anyway, despite the fact that it must have been something of a letdown. For Marilyn, being Marilyn, did what she always seemed to do: she absorbed all the available light and made it her own.

When she was there—on-screen, or in person—it became almost impossible to pay attention to anyone else. And maybe that, more than anything, was her special gift: the riveting of the collective attention to one face, one form, one voice, as it smiled and moved and utterly transformed everything around it.

I was too young to have known or appreciated the phenomenon that was Marilyn Monroe firsthand: I was five years old when she died on that August morning in 1962. But I can remember quite vividly the first televised image I saw of her: a clip of the now-famous rendition of "Happy Birthday" she sang for President John F. Kennedy. She wore a sparkling, beaded gown that seemed quite transparent, and beneath it, little or perhaps even nothing else. The spotlight quivered and dipped but was essentially confined to her radiant face; it never moved below, so that her nearly naked breasts and body remained in a kind of tantalizing shadow. Who would not be tantalized by her performance, this beautiful woman with the little-girl voice who embodied so many different kinds of resonant and unsettling paradoxes?

The facts of her life are, at this point, familiar signposts in the well-rehearsed legend. Born to Gladys Pearl Baker in Los Angeles on June 1, 1926, the name on her

4    birth certificate is Norma Jeane. Her father is nowhere
in sight and her mother is soon diagnosed as a paranoid
schizophrenic. After a brief stint in an orphanage, little
Norma Jeane is bounced around from foster home to
foster home. She marries a local neighbor boy at sixteen, embarks on a modeling career, and is soon discovered by a Hollywood movie executive. The husband is
discarded, like so much else in her earlier life. In 1947, at
the age of twenty-one, she appeared in her first motion
picture; by 1950, her roles in such films as *The Asphalt
Jungle* and *All About Eve* begin to command attention.
There are more films, of course, and eventually she
achieves starring roles in them: *Gentlemen Prefer Blondes,
How to Marry a Millionaire, The Seven Year Itch, Bus Stop,
Some Like It Hot.* There are well-publicized marriages,
to ballplayer Joe DiMaggio and playwright Arthur
Miller, and equally well-publicized divorces. And there
are affairs, lots of them, with other movie stars, like Yves
Montand, or with politicians, like the Kennedys. There
are nervous breakdowns, bouts of depression, miscarriages, and suicide attempts. Finally, there is the drug
overdose—intentional? accidental?—and on August 5,
1962, Marilyn's lovely light went out forever.

But in fact, this is hardly what happened. If anything,
the legend that is Marilyn Monroe has even surpassed
the life. For one thing, there are the films, and film
grants a kind of immortality in the face of all the evidence to the contrary. Even though we may know, intel-

lectually, that Marilyn Monroe died by her own hand from an overdose of barbiturates, when her violet-satin-clad body—seen in a series of mirrors—spans the screen five times over in *How to Marry a Millionaire,* or when her creamy, abundant flesh pours, once more, from the low-cut black negligee she wears in *Some Like It Hot,* she is with us still; she lives.

Hollywood has had its share of icons and sacrifices before and after her: James Dean, Carol Lombard, Jayne Mansfield, all had tragic and untimely deaths. But more than any other, Marilyn's is the story that continues to weave itself around our collective consciousness. Forty years later, she continues to captivate and compel, offering some elusive glimpse—perhaps it is a mirror, perhaps a window—into the soul of the life and times that traipsed on without her.

The essays in this book attempt to come to grips with her ongoing power to fascinate, to entrance, and to inspire. Some are taken from already existing material, for Marilyn's life and death prompted responses and analyses from any number of notable writers. Others were commissioned expressly for this volume and address what has happened in the forty years since she walked among us, the gap, as it were, between the reality—which of course we will never know—and the fantasy that has assumed an intricate and engaging pattern all its own. Marilyn—both the woman and the myth—remains at the center of it all.

*all the available light*

# freeze frame:
## monroe as icon

The concept of Monroe as an icon goes straight to the heart of the matter; by now, we are more familiar with her iconic status than with almost anything else about her. How many people have actually seen *The Seven Year Itch*? But how many haven't seen its most famous promotional image, that of Monroe standing over the subway grating as the whoosh of air lifts her skirt skyward? And that is only one of the many visual signposts she has left behind.

It could be said that the photographs remain the most enduring aspect of Monroe's legacy. She had to be one of the most photographed individuals of the twentieth century, and certainly one of the most photogenic. Forty years after her death, the hundreds—no, thousands—of pictures continue to fascinate, enchant, and arouse. Her image is everywhere, blown-up on posters and billboards, reduced and trivialized on coffee mugs, T-shirts, postcards, and even rubber stamps. The two essays in this section squarely address the iconic status Monroe has assumed.

In "Iconomania," Richard Woodward—whose essays on photography have appeared in a slew of national publications—examines, in minute detail, three of the central images that form the Monroe constellation: the famous calendar pinup, the publicity shot from *The Seven Year Itch,* and a silkscreen by Andy Warhol. It is telling that so many other writers—both within this collection and outside its boundaries—have chosen to comment on these same images. But Woodward's reading—especially of the publicity shot—offers a new level of complexity to an already indelible photograph.

In Joyce Carol Oates's "Centerfold," we are literally given a glimpse inside the famous calendar image, the one that went on to become the very first *Playboy* pinup. American woman of letters Oates has had a long fascination with Monroe; the recent publication of her novel, *Blonde,* is the culmination of that interest. In the previously unpublished essay that appears here, Oates assumes Monroe's voice—and in so doing, her persona—to deconstruct the famous picture.

Read together, these pieces begin to shape a definition of Monroe in the twenty-first century, one that is in great part comprised of the moments she spent before the camera's rapt and insatiable gaze.

## ICONOMANIA: SEX, DEATH, PHOTOGRAPHY, AND THE MYTH OF MARILYN MONROE
*Richard B. Woodward*

*W*alker Evans, that most egalitarian of snobs, invariably turned up his nose at commissions to photograph famous people. Celebrity portraiture was, in his withering phrase, nothing more than "photographic name-dropping." He and his friend James Agee loved to ridicule Edward Steichen, Margaret Bourke-White, and other eminent vulgarians of the day who earned their handsome incomes and illustrious reputations by glamorizing the fashionable and the well-to-do.

With ambitions for photography at once more humble and more exalted, Evans found journalistic toadying before the goddess of fame to be beneath his dignity as an artist. He thought highly of himself but, in keeping with his taste for the plain and overlooked aspects of American life, preferred to keep a low profile. He was a stickler for self-effacing manners and held himself at a studious distance from his subjects. His shy, aristocratic temperament could not abide the aggressive mutual exploitation at the heart of most celebrity transactions. He loathed art laden with political or commercial messages, and celebrity photography is bloated with both. It would not exist, in fact, without them.

What's more, the inherent laziness built into the process of making and appreciating such portraits didn't agree with his puritanical nature. It hardly matters if a photographer glorifies or belittles a famous person; the heavy lifting that gives artistic weight to a picture has already been done by someone else. It is the luster of the celebrity that dazzles the viewer and has enticed a third party, usually a magazine or newspaper, to commission the picture in the first place. These third parties have on hand a series of ready-made narratives into which the figures are cast—hottest young restaurant designer in San Francisco, ingenue-to-watch in new Hollywood blockbuster, triumphant general returned from war—and which determine the reading of the picture. The photographer is left with the relatively minor task of illustrating the same set of tired old stories.

Marilyn Monroe must have confirmed Evans's worst fears about famous people and those who portrayed them. It didn't seem to matter how often and with what intentions men and women looked at her through a lens; her stardom ultimately overwhelmed them. She was—and still is—the supernova of American postwar celebrities against which all others are measured. No photographer had a chance of finding the light outside the brilliance she cast. Even other celebrities, including her two last eminent husbands, found themselves overshadowed. The tabloid story of her life, with its well-worn chapters and pitiful end, tints the meaning of every photograph taken of her. We are far more eager to judge these images according to whatever hints they may contain about a particular phase of Monroe's life than we are to grant them status as works of art. Their art is that they are imprinted with the image of Marilyn.

And yet the fusion of the two—the badly written Hollywood script that her life has become and the images that chronicle her sad rise and fall—produced certain icons, or visual clichés, that people everywhere remember. She was a photographer's dream, happy to pose and feed the camera's hungry eye. The substance of her life seems to exist now in publicity stills and celluloid flashes, so much so it's hard to think of her as flesh and bone. She is one of the few true goddesses of the cinema, able to confer the blessing of long life and special value on everything she may have touched, from dresses to teapots. That the culture still needs her, and has sanctified her (along with Elvis) in this way, transforming certain images of her into international icons, is itself significant and has added a weirdly fascinating postscript to her life. In fact, the story of Marilyn after death is in many ways even more peculiar than the story of Marilyn alive.

LASTING RENOWN IS incalculably rarer than fifteen minutes of fame. Most of everything ever raised off the ground has vanished with barely a trace or sigh of regret. Countless structures have gone up around the world during the last six thousand years: palaces, huts, forts, temples, igloos, altars, bridges, outhouses, factories, office towers, shopping malls, doghouses, and drive-in movie theaters. And yet by the next millennium, the overwhelming number of things on the earth today will be hard to find or even recall.

Time isn't any kinder to living things. The faceless and nameless multitudes vastly outnumber the immortals of history. For every Cleopatra celebrated in art and verse, several hundred thousand women lived and died unsung and anonymous during the reign of the Ptolemies. No schoolchild can avoid a lesson on Napoleon. But how many learn anything about the half-million or so common soldiers he led? They are remembered now, if at all, as tiny print in the lower branches of French family trees.

*all the available light*

The grinding forces of time and changing social concerns mercilessly sift anything that might be of value or interest to the present from those people or things regarded as useless or hopelessly antiquated. Millions of photographs were shot during the decades of the Vietnam War. But a few images—a Buddhist monk who has set himself on fire, a man being shot in the head in the street, and a screaming Vietnamese girl running naked down a road—are icons of that time. They are remembered by anyone who lived through those years, even when the photographers (Malcolm Browne, Eddie Adams, and Huynh Cong Ut) are not.

One of the tests for someone or something to qualify as an icon—a term so debased by overuse that it needs to be sparingly applied—should be the fifty-year rule. Is the person still famous half a century after death? Has time diminished or magnified the original notoriety? In the case of a building, painting, sculpture, or photograph, is it better known today than when first constructed or seen? Or have reproductions of it faded from view?

Monroe is a legitimate icon on several counts, not least of which is her increasing renown, especially when judged against her peers. Among actors of the postwar era, only John Wayne and James Dean come close to enjoying her posthumous fame around the world. Has any actress inspired more imitators—everyone from Madonna, to flavor-of-the-month sex goddesses, to a thousand drag queens with platinum bouffant wigs, sequined gowns, and a facial mole painted on with mascara? Even if the "Hollywood blonde" was invented by Dietrich and Harlow, Monroe stole and perfected the look, adding an attitude that, depending on your sexual politics, is either cluelessly or ironically dumb.

One reason that Monroe is imprinted so clearly on the public mind is photography. As well as any figure of her time, she seemed to have understood that—at least in the celluloid world where she had staked her claim—one's picture could be used like currency, traded freely to help everyone involved earn money and fame. Unlike many of today's movie actors with their strict control over who portrays them and where these photographs shall appear, she was throughout her life unguarded about, even promiscuous with, images of herself. She courted notoriety and benefited from a profitably corrupt yet also largely innocent partnership with any number of photographers, André de Dienes to Richard Avedon. Photography slingshot her into an orbit all her own as perhaps the world's most recognized woman when she was alive.

Certain of these images—and by no means those taken by the best photographers; in fact, quite the reverse—have solidified into icons, ensuring that she is as famous today as she was at her death forty years ago.

Lasting fame is not automatically bestowed on the most photographed. It is one thing to have your picture taken millions of times, as has happened to, say, Gerald

Ford and John Major. Whatever historians may decide about their legacy, pro or con, they will likely suffer the same photographic fate that has befallen Warren Harding and Herbert Asquith. People a century from now will be hard-pressed to identify them without a caption. To call Ford or Major an icon would be a misnomer when their newsprint likenesses already seem to be disappearing.

It is quite another thing when the same few pictures of you are reproduced again and again, as happened to Monroe. Among the thousands of portraits taken, a select group overwhelm the rest in popularity. Reproduced on postage stamps, billboards, postcards, book covers, as diner decor, sidewalk sculpture in New York, or casino souvenirs in Las Vegas, these few images have made her as common a sight in Sydney as in Rio de Janeiro. Her face and body embalmed in the public's memory, Monroe can be called, for the present anyway, an immortal on the scale of Napoleon or Cleopatra.

These few photographs are now as well known as her movies, if not more so. Tom Kelley's full-length nudes of the out-of-work actress, stretched across a rippling sea of red velvet, may be the most celebrated pinups in history. Far more people know the stills of the laughing blonde standing over a New York subway grating, her white skirt billowing at her waist, than have ever seen the *The Seven Year Itch*. However much Monroe may have owed to Billy Wilder while she was alive, her posthumous fame is now linked to Andy Warhol's, whose *Marilyn Monroe* series is among the most commonly reproduced works of art from the late twentieth century.

The process of icon formation is often hard to explain. The social forces that over time select and preserve one picture or thing or person from among 10 million are ruthless, and seemingly fickle. Why have Cary Grant or Bette Davis left behind no iconic images for posterity on a par with Monroe's? Why should the Taj Mahal, hardly the most ancient or grandest building in Asia, be the best known? Why do the Vietnam photographs by Browne, Adams, and Ut surpass in recognition all others from that time?

One can only make plausible guesses why certain objects congeal into clichés. In his absorbing book *Inventing Leonardo,* art historian Richard Turner traces the many converging factors that led to the *Mona Lisa*'s becoming, perhaps, the icon of icons. The portrait was, first of all, innovative in technique, its chiaroscuro and triangular composition widely admired and imitated. Although kept under wraps in France after 1510 and unavailable except to a few artists until the seventeenth century, many copies circulated and Vasari singled it out for lavish praise in his *Lives of the Artists,* published in 1565.

After the French Revolution, the painting ended up in the collections of the government in the Musée du Louvre. With the nineteenth-century Romantics celebrating Leonardo as the archetype of universal genius, *La Gioconda* occupied a hallowed place in his small but

18 highly venerated oeuvre. The anonymous woman depicted in this simple portrait—referred to as a "masterpiece" for the first time during this period—began to excite myriad fantasies about her relationship to the artist. Men began to project their fears about women as well as their fevered desires about art onto this painted icon. Her quiet smile proved she had seduced Leonardo (or was it the other way around?). Walter Pater composed a poem that likened her to a vampire. She was a siren, an enchantress who had enslaved the greatest mind of the Renaissance. As a topper, in a 1910 essay, Freud proposed that the work revealed clues about Leonardo's troubled feelings toward his mother. The essay became a paradigm for future efforts at psychobiography. Then, in 1911, the *Mona Lisa* was stolen from the Louvre in what was probably the biggest art story of the century. Many books were written and at least two feature movies made about the theft. Finally, in 1919, Duchamp added facial hair and a dirty title (in a coded pun, as secret as the lady's smile) to a postcard reproduction of the painting, an act of graffiti that both mocked its status as a "classic" for the general populace and as a maternal figure for the Freudians. Duchamp's parody has even become a parasitic icon all its own, inspiring hundreds of knockoffs and further reinforcing the painting's present rank as the mother of clichés.

Nothing can fully explain why hordes of tourists at the Louvre, whether arriving from China or Des Moines, race single-mindedly toward one painting. But these historical and ideological clues do suggest how Leonardo's lady could have become so famous that she epitomizes "art" for much of the world. Turner shows that these busloads of people weren't by any means the first to be fixated and they certainly won't be the last.

Marilyn Monroe may not be a painting, but her life has been treated like a canvas where for decades writers, male and female, have splashed colorful fantasies about her illegitimate birth, lonely childhood, career, marriages, affairs, death, and lasting stardom as freely as Freud had with the *Mona Lisa.* Like any icon, Marilyn is as symbolic as she is real. What she represents is by now as telling—about us, anyway—as anything she actually did. Myths about love and death stand behind the formation of many icons, including the Taj Mahal and the Pyramids, and the pictures of Monroe known far and wide suggest that sexual desires and taboos have everything to do with their special status, and hers. Her synonymy with "sex," like the *Mona Lisa's* with "art," is so pervasive that the mention of her name often bores those who detest clichés of any kind.

In all likelihood, Monroe's career would never have taken off, nor would she be long remembered, had she not posed nude for commercial photographer Tom Kelley in his Los Angeles studio on May 27, 1949. The facts of the story have themselves been retold so often they have taken on their own mythic character. Four days shy of her twenty-third birthday, Monroe, in need of money to meet her rent and car payments, approached Kelley and offered to model. She had already done a clothed session with him in early May that resulted in a poster for Pabst that attracted the notice of the beer's advertising agency. According to Donald Spoto, one of Monroe's most dogged biographers, Kelley was renowned for having "produced some of the most aesthetically pleasing camera art of that time" and for his "innovative approaches to the presentation of humans with products." (Other biographers have been less kind. Barbara Leaming dismisses Kelley as a "cheesecake photographer" and the pictures themselves don't receive much scrutiny in her book.)

The May 27 shoot was a commission from a Chicago calendar manufacturer who distributed the items to garages, car dealers, and other businesses frequented mainly by men. The session called for Monroe to be nude and, although the name she signed on the release ("Mara Monroe") indicates she was not completely proud of herself, she threw herself into the job, according to Kelley's recollections. He put on one of Monroe's favorite records, Artie Shaw's "Begin the Beguine," and they went to work. In a couple of hours, Kelley shot dozens of pictures. But only two of these poses—kitschily titled *A New Wrinkle* and *Golden Dreams* for the calendar—survive from that day. Even so, it is probably not much of an exaggeration to say they are among the best-known photographs of their kind—and for good reason.

They caused an earthquake in the American media before they were seen. News of their very existence was enough to shake up Hollywood, with reverberations that were felt in Washington, D.C. And when finally published and republished—in magazines, books of pin-ups, biographies of Monroe—and when the dust settled and the reaction to the story could be assessed, these two nude pictures proved to have been instrumental in changing, perhaps forever, the nation's attitude toward sex, nudity, publicity, and stardom.

By contemporary pornographic standards, they are artistic nudes, almost chaste in what they don't dare to reveal. *A New Wrinkle,* in which she is stretched out on a rippling sea of red velvet, shows her in profile, her dark blond hair spread out like a Japanese fan around her head, and with one of her red nipples protruding; *Golden Dreams* is frontal, more carnal, with both breasts proudly displayed and her knees coyly turned in a pose that defined the limits of risqué for many years in the skin magazines until the "Pubic Wars" between *Penthouse* and *Playboy* during the 1970s.

Monroe claimed to have forgotten about the pictures by 1952 when Twentieth Century-Fox learned that the young actress, under contract since 1950, was also appearing around the country as a naked calendar girl for grease monkeys. The media insanity—analogous to the storm that buffeted Vanessa Williams in 1984, when *Penthouse* published old photographs of the new Miss America enjoying simulated lesbian sex in the nude—was carefully managed by the studio and by Monroe herself, in consultation with her advisor, Sidney Skolsky. Anthony Summers, in his book *Goddess: The Secret Lives of Marilyn Monroe*, tells how the contrite actress smoothly leaked news of the photographs and the calendar to a woman reporter from UPI, who wrote a sympathetic story that went national on March 13, 1952. It portrayed Marilyn as a victim: she had needed money and been paid only $50 for the pictures—a figure that has turned up in nearly every subsequent account.

The strategy worked, and then some. She was just another aspiring starlet before the photographs popped up; soon afterward she was known as a sex goddess, and has been ever since. The images sent a frisson through the culture. In early 1953, a camera-store owner in Los Angeles was arrested after boys were seen ogling the calendar in his window, and it was officially banned in Pennsylvania and Georgia. But the scandal only boosted her fame. That overseer of public morals, J. Edgar Hoover, reportedly hung a copy in his office.

Monroe in the guise of these newly minted icons turned up on cocktail napkins, bar glasses, pens, key chains, and playing cards. By the time *Golden Dreams* was chosen as the first centerfold in the first issue of *Playboy,* in December 1953—the twenty-seven-year old publisher Hugh Hefner paid Kelley $500 to reprint the image, and put a clothed Monroe on the cover—she had been transformed into a commodity who could sell magazines to heterosexual men. It could be argued that the *Playboy* empire, with all of the social changes it has brought to the world, was built on this image. Through no plan of her own, Monroe revolutionized the country's attitudes toward nudity and self-promotion. She was the first actress to prove that taking off your clothes for *Playboy* can amplify your career, not end it. Hundreds of unknowns ever since have disrobed for photographers in the hopes of becoming as famous as Monroe; and dozens of celebrities, from Kim Basinger and Katerina Witt to Sharon Stone and Darva Conger, have made the same calculation as a strategy for breaking into Hollywood. The raunchy pictures of Vanessa Williams, hurtful when first published, also ensured her international headlines for weeks. How many other Miss Americas from the 1980s can you name?

*Golden Dreams* and *A New Wrinkle* were not only the first photographs of a naked woman that many American males in the 1950s ever saw, they were almost certainly the first naked pictures of a celebrity. To see barebreasted aboriginals in *National Geographic* was more of an anthropologic than an erotic experience. But to gaze at a Hollywood star without a stitch on, even if she looked too young in 1949 to correspond to the platinum-haired fleshpot who had wowed you in the theater and in *Life* magazine, was to have a dream threesome: sex and fame and you. No wonder, then, that Monroe's calendar

*all the available light*

photographs have remained icons. For the history of censorship and sexual politics in America, they are documents as crucial and fracturing as *Lady Chatterly's Lover* and *Deep Throat*.

For women, the pictures are less well remembered. Many fewer saw them in the 1950s. The photographs weren't made for their eyes nor, despite recent marketing efforts, was *Playboy*. Many women who chanced upon them in their husband's or son's closets felt unfriendly toward Monroe. The buying and selling of women for sex has too odious a history for some people to look anywhere but askance at someone who takes off her clothes for money. The $50 that Monroe received for the session is likely seen by women as proof that she was, as she claimed, a victim and grossly underpaid. Men can agree about the injustice but also recognize the sum as what one would pay for a standard illicit sexual transaction with a prostitute. She is the mythical $50 hooker. The pictures have left a gender gap among Marilyn's biographers as well. Norman Mailer features one of the calendar pictures in his essay. But neither of the women with prominent books about her—Gloria Steinem and Barbara Leaming—included the nude shot, although it appears as a jigsaw puzzle in the background with other objects made from Marilyn's face and body in Steinem's chapter called "The Woman Who Will Not Die." [Editor's note: This chapter is reprinted elsewhere in this volume without the pictures.]

But the most popular photographs of Monroe by far, known to as many women as men, are those taken during the subway updraft scene in *The Seven Year Itch*. The outrageous blond exhibitionist—white skirt swirling around her hips, and portions of her white panties exposed—defines Marilyn for much of the world, if any one image can. Reproduced everywhere in plaster and neon, as cardboard cutouts and painted murals, the picture ranks among the most recognizable of the late twentieth century.

It was not a spontaneous snapshot but part of a carefully planned campaign to take advantage of Monroe's recent notoriety as a sexual libertine. According to Leaming's biography, photographer Sam Shaw had taken a picture in 1941 of sailors with their girlfriends at the Steeplechase in Coney Island for *Friday* magazine. The cover featured one of the women with her skirt blown up by a gust of air. Shaw, who was a friend of Monroe and also at work on a documentary about the making of *The Seven Year Itch,* convinced Twentieth Century-Fox and director Billy Wilder that this same suggestive pose, with Monroe enjoying the urban breezes, should be the centerpiece of the movie's publicity.

For days before the scene was to be filmed on September, 15, 1954, the New York newspapers had been printing photographs of Monroe and issuing regular alerts on her whereabouts. The *Daily News* dubbed her "a roadblock called Marilyn." Crowds attended the shooting of every scene they could get near. At two in the morning when midtown Manhattan is usually deserted, thousands of people, including dozens of photographers, were hanging around East 55th Street for the chance of seeing Monroe during the subway scene. They were not disappointed.

Elements in the story of what happened next may not be entirely true but, even if not, help to explain the mythic aura that has sustained the photographs in public memory. There were many takes (and camera flashes) as the wind machine underneath the subway grating on Lexington Avenue blew up Monroe's skirt. She wore no stockings and, according to several accounts, her two pairs of sheer nylon panties did not hide everything. Leaming writes that the onlookers kept shouting "'Let's see more!' There was oddly little pretense of keeping people quiet. On the contrary, the numerous takes seemed calculated to work up the crowd and to guarantee that magazines and newspapers would print a great many pictures of Marilyn in her panties. The entire evening was a spectacular publicity stunt."

One horrified observer of the scene was her husband, Joe DiMaggio, who had been dragged there late from Toots Shor's by columnist Walter Winchell. After watching his wife's behavior in front of the cameras and how she indulged the crowd, swiveling her hips and laughing at the wolf whistles, oblivious to her nether translucency, DiMaggio stormed off in a rage. He was humiliated. There are many stories of a nasty fight between the couple that night in their hotel. Two weeks later, they announced the separation that led to their divorce. Photography, then, helped to shatter the marriage between the sports hero and the screen goddess.

DiMaggio could not have objected to the much-less-revealing version of the subway scene shot later back in Hollywood, in which her skirt never rises above her knees. This is the subway scene cut into the final print of the movie. But the hundreds of publicity stills that ran in magazines and newspapers around the world were, within limits, much more titillating. The image was hard to miss. A gigantic Marilyn, fifty feet high, towered over Times Square during the film's release. The image has petrified into an icon, outliving the media frenzy that created it, because it is so charged with meanings, chiefly the myth of Marilyn as angelic whore. If not a dirty picture, it is undeniably hot. The expression of pleasure etched on her face and body can only be called orgasmic. She seems to be enjoying a sexual act, with us and with herself, in the middle of a New York street. Exposing her most private anatomy to the viewer, she seems not to mind if we indulge in fantasies of getting into her pants. She is an urban goddess, straddling the subway grating while the New York masses, disguised as a gust of wind, look up her dress from underground; and she is such a generous and powerful goddess that the people from below, the workingmen who ride the subway, are allowed to have sex with her.

It is also a historic image, one that destroyed a marriage consecrated in American tabloid heaven. Celebrities should gravitate toward one another, according to the popular press, and then, if all goes well, break up in an explosive scandal, complete with photographs. In this sad farce of love and fame, Joe and Marilyn seemed to know their roles by heart. There were also rumors of undoctored pictures that circulated among those with connections. To see a Hollywood star's pubic hair in 1954—as several accounts claim was possible during the five hours of filming that night—trumped one of the taboos not yet transgressed in the calendar pictures. Sneaking a peek at the crotch of the glamorous wife, who belonged to the most revered sports star in America, gave any man a sense of power. Anyone who laughed at or fantasized about this picture was in a sense cuckolding DiMaggio.

But like so many pictures of the mature Monroe, the pose is also a knowing and innocent tease, a risqué joke, a hoot. Girls just want to have fun, don't they? She is getting off on our getting off, but both parties are aware it's a performance. She is dressed head-to-toe in white—white earrings, white dress, white underwear, white shoes—no doubt as a studio ploy to throw off the censors. (Were she dressed in red, the outrageousness of the scene might be more glaring.) But the symbolism of the outfit also lends an ethereal air to the burlesque of undressing in front of strangers. In some versions of the image—and there are dozens—the skirt flies up like a pair of wings, even if they seem attached to her hips. Profane and holy, the picture is a composite of Marilyn the carnal angel.

DESPITE POSING IN front of the camera hundreds of times, for walls of flashbulbs at studio-sponsored publicity events and in one-on-one sessions with the likes of Richard Avedon, Milton Greene, Eve Arnold, and Bert Stern, Monroe was the kind of star whose luminescence outshined everyone who photographed her. They could share in her fame, but it was hers to bestow. Billy Wilder's observation—"the first day a photographer took a picture of her she was a genius"—is a rueful admission of her superiority over anyone who hoped to capture her on film. Many took advantage of the opportunity for reflected glory. The pile of posthumous photography books attests to the bankability of her name, even if the texts say more about the parasitic nature of celebrity journalism than they do about Monroe.

"Making love and making photographs were closely connected in my mind when it came to women," Stern writes with more lecherous candor than seems necessary. He confesses that in their two sessions he couldn't wait to entice her out of her clothes but that gallantry prevented him from falling into bed with her. His high morals, of course, did not prevent him from publishing the nudes from their last session, which Monroe hated so much that she defaced many of the negatives with a hairpin.

As a woman, Arnold is more protective and less smitten. She realizes that Monroe exploited her for publicity, cozying up to the *Life* photographer in order to project a fresher, less salacious persona to the world. But Arnold isn't bitter; that's the way the game is played. "I never knew anyone who even came close to Marilyn in natural ability to use both photographer and still camera," she writes. "She would pose for almost anybody who had a box Brownie with the same grace and skill she gave to professionals." Although the photographers complain about one another—Stern carps about Avedon, Arnold snipes at Stern—all of them seem to have adored Marilyn.

Andy Warhol may be the only artist who was a match for Monroe. He was not unlike her in several respects. They were both nobodies who climbed to the top by manipulating images. Like her, he was a master of passivity, absorbing energy from others. He loved celebrity just as hungrily as she and was shrewd enough to grasp the duplicity of fame: how someone—especially a photographer—could become famous by putting famous people and things in his work. He liked to have his picture taken almost as much as she did, and he ended up— with his trademark pale skin, blank expression, and platinum wig—as one of the best-known artists of the century, an icon himself.

But his art was as cool as she was hot. His prints from

photographs were antiexpressionist, antipsychological, anti–Method acting. *Gold Marilyn Monroe* from 1962 seems at first to be anti-Marilyn. There is no sign of ardor or innocence or fun. It isn't a flattering portrait. Bodiless, she has been robbed of some of her best-known assets. The makeup on her eyes and lips is smeared so that she looks like a floozy, or a drag queen on drugs. Warhol doesn't hint at an inner life for the actress or pretend that an image can express a sad childhood or foreshadow suicide.

Which is why it's an icon. When so many of the photographs by professionals hope to peek beneath the glamour—and fail—*Gold Marilyn Monroe* succeeds because Warhol respected surfaces. Rather than removing her makeup and mask, he made an image out of little else. He had no desire to steer Monroe toward the bedroom, or to protect her. His interest was strictly business. The superficial realities of life—celebrities, fashion, society, and glamour—were for Warhol the bottom line. It's no accident that in this cynical homage to Hollywood, an altar where a gay man and a voluptuous sexpot could worship together, he slathered the blond screen star in gold, the cliché of wealth. Like Auric Goldfinger, Warhol craved money more than sex. But even if he portrayed her as the whore of Hollywood Babylon or a tarted-up Byzantine icon, he also clearly revered her as a trashy American goddess. The picture suggests that fame is often as opaque as saintliness.

Monroe had no children, nor did Warhol. But both have countless offspring who play around in various media with photography and fame; Madonna and Cindy Sherman are their progeny and have spawned their own numberless imitators.

The huge array of image-makers and outlets for images, though, has made it much harder for any one picture to solidify into an icon. The jittery pace of reading and absorbing images is now set by the trigger finger on a TV remote or computer mouse rather than by a slow hand turning a page. Madonna achieved fame with videos on television, not via naked photographs in calendars or magazines. Although the uproar over the discovery of her youthful nudes—which were later published in *Playboy* and *Penthouse*—echoed eerily like Monroe's, no one picture of Madonna then or since has become an icon. Princess Diana was the most photographed person in the world. Her adult life can be found in a stream of images locked away in photo-agency archives. But at her death no one picture popped up on television or in magazines more than any other.

Despite invocations of Monroe in Elton John's maudlin funeral ode, Diana's life seems too insubstantial to have impressed itself on the culture in the form of an icon; and without relics to keep memory aflame, the myth often goes up in smoke.

Diana was born as the age of the photograph was passing away, succeeded in the sixties by the fifteen-second film or video clip. Vietnam became the last photographic war as well as the first to be televised. The Zapruder footage of the Kennedy assassination, watched and analyzed endlessly, kicked off the era of amateur surveillance. News events, like the *Challenger* explosion, the O.J. Simpson Bronco chase, the Rodney King beatings, or Diana's final minutes, are replayed more memorably in tape loops on electronic screens rather than as still images on paper. It was telling that in the plane-crash coverage of JFK, Jr., a man hounded all his life by photographers, the one image repeated over and over dated back to 1963: the child saluting his father's casket.

Monroe thrived during the glory years of photography and she died as they were fading. The only images from the last year of her life that have retained the iconic potency of earlier ones are a few seconds of moving pictures: the clip from the tribute to JFK at Madison Square Garden on May 19, 1962. Rolled out invariably whenever anyone tries to tell the life story of either the soon-to-be slain president or the soon-to-be suicidal movie star, it is the moment that unites them. As she shimmies in her sequined gown toward the spotlight to sing in her breathiest voice, "Happy Birthday, Mr. President," her quirky sense of timing, sweet way with an innuendo, and her love affair with American celebrity and power are captured perfectly by the camera. Like those few seconds in which a more recent American leader wades into a crowd on the White House lawn and em-

*all the available light*

34    braces a young woman in a beret, Marilyn crooning to
Jack and his friends can be rewound again and again as
we search for hints of sexual misdeeds, future or past,
that we know must be there.

If love and death provide the richest ores for myth-
making, Monroe's life was the mother lode. Future gen-
erations may not need her to embody their illicit desires
as much as did Cold War America. But there seems to
be no shortage of events or characters in the past, present, and foreseeable future for which her name will not
deserve to be summoned up, even if it's only to help us
tell a real gilded icon from a fake.

CENTERFOLD

*Joyce Carol Oates*

     *H*ello, there! What's your name? I'm Miss Golden Dreams—Marilyn Monroe. Actually, I wasn't Marilyn yet, I was Norma Jeane Baker. Twenty-three when this to-be-famous nude calendar photo was taken one desperate afternoon in Los Angeles, in 1949. My picture—usually in a bathing suit!—had been on the cover of magazines like *Swank, YANK, Stars and Stripes, Peek,* but I couldn't get modeling assignments and I'd been dropped as a "starlet" by two major Hollywood studios and my secondhand car had just been repossessed by the finance company and I needed just $50 to get it back—and $50 was what I was paid for this pose, which would earn millions of dollars for other people. For men. But I'm not bitter! I'm History: the first *Playboy* center-fold, "Sweetheart of the Month" for November 1953, and I was on the cover, too! Marilyn Monroe and *Playboy* magazine—what a combination! Do you think I'm beautiful? desirable? lovable? How'd you like to love me? I know I could love *you*. I was desperate for love all my life, especially when I was Norma Jeane and only a naive girl in Hollywood. Always, I've believed that if a woman isn't loved by a man, she isn't *anything*. I'd been married at 16, a virgin, and my young husband left me to go overseas in the Merchant Marine. He loved me, I think—but I needed so much love, continuous, reassuring love, it was too much for him! I guess I just wanted to "cuddle" all the time, and make love! I called my husband "Daddy" though he was only five years older than me. This was in 1945. When he was shipped out—by his request—to Australia, I threatened to kill myself—I begged him to make me pregnant—but he left anyway, and my heart was broken. *You* wouldn't break my heart, would you? I believe that the human body, nude, is beautiful. I've never been ashamed of posing nude. All my shyness went away when I removed my clothes! Sex is nature—and I'm all for nature, aren't you? Just look at my perfect body, I love you looking at me. Don't stop! It's true—I was never ashamed or embarrassed of my body, even as a child. My body was my "Magic Friend"—it would make me loved, it would make people take note of me. I'd dream of taking off my clothes even in church—naked in the eyes of God and man! But deformity and ugliness frighten me, I never want to get old and ugly. It wasn't a lie, only just a strategy. I told people I was an orphan who hadn't known her parents but in fact I knew my mother—she'd had nervous breakdowns and was institutionalized for most of her life. I never knew my father—he refused to acknowledge me even after I became MARILYN MONROE, and famous! He broke my heart, too, I guess—but I try not to be bitter. Nobody wants a broody Sweetheart of the Month, do they?—*I* wouldn't, myself! Could you guess seeing me here so young, so sweet and vulnerable, that in a few years I'd be internationally famous as MARILYN MONROE, the #1 Sex Symbol of the 20th Century? I loved every minute of it, it was my revenge, and we know—revenge is sweet! After my husband left me I did defense work in an airplane factory in Van Nuys and there I was photographed by a roving reporter for *Stars and Stripes*—just by chance! And my entire life was changed. Out of nowhere there I was suddenly on a magazine cover, and my photo really caught the public's eye—I mean, men's eyes. My tight sweaters and coveralls really attracted attention and in no time at all I quit my job and became a "photographer's model"—in tight sweaters, skirts, and swimsuits like Betty Grable, who was THE pin-up of World War II.

*all the available light*

Except I was sexier than Betty Grable ever was, my "vital statistics" (37-22-38) were more impressive than hers and I was always more mysterious, and desirable—don't you think? Men were crazy to love me—but maybe, too, to hurt me. My appeal wasn't just my creamy-pale perfect skin, or my open-mouthed glossy-red smile I'd practiced to perfection, or my baby-breathy voice and liquidy blue eyes—my appeal was, I lived in your unconscious! And I'm living there still more than four decades after my death. *That's* something to be proud of. (Except I was always hurt—more than hurt, damned angry—that I was exploited by Twentieth Century-Fox executives through most of my career. I was a contract actress—a slave. I'd signed contracts when I was desperate, and while I was earning millions for the studio they were paying me $1,500 a week. I was the blonde of *Gentlemen Prefer Blondes,* but I earned far less than my co-star Jane Russell. At the height of my career, I was paid $100,000 for a movie—while Elizabeth Taylor, my contemporary and rival, was paid $1 million by the studio. When I tried to rebel, they hated me. When I died, 13 years after GOLDEN DREAMS, my body lay unclaimed in the Los Angeles morgue for several days because my savings and estate were so modest, no one wanted to make the commitment to pay for my funeral expenses— until my ex-husband Joe DiMaggio came forward. (*He* loved me, even if we couldn't live with each other.) "No sex is wrong if there's love in it"—do you think so, too? That's my credo! Just like the naked human body, sex is beautiful and nothing to be ashamed of—yes? At least, if you're a beautiful, desirable woman—and young. This photo of me became famous through the world—NOTORI-OUS! The calendar—which was almost banned from the U.S. mail as "pornographic"—sold millions of copies, and is selling still. (There are other poses of me against this sensuous red velvet backdrop in which you can see just a little of my pubic hair—these I preferred as "more honest." But pubic hair couldn't be displayed on a calendar in 1949!) It helped launch the premiere issue of a fantastic new magazine, *Playboy,* edited by an adventurous, idealistic twenty-seven-year-old named Hugh Hefner, a magazine for men that in the straitlaced, puritanical, and hypocritical fifties dared to celebrate sexual freedom and sexual health and the sexualized beauty of the female body. I'm proud of this, I think. Well—I know I should have asked for a contract to pay me royalties for future sales of this photo, but as I said, I was desperate for cash, and $50 looked good to me. (The photographer sold the negative for $500!) But all this talk of money is misleading, actually—I never cared much for money, and only slept with Hollywood producers and executives to help me with my career, never for money or gifts. (Don't frown: you would have done the same thing in my place. Every young starlet did!) But I never slept with any man for money, and when a wealthy agent wanted to marry me, I refused. Everyone thought I was crazy and maybe I was but— "I will only marry for love!" I said. And that was so: I married three times for love, and each marriage

*all the available light*

ended in divorce. But would I marry again, now? I would! I'm your first *Playboy* centerfold—please can I be your last? If you like what you see here, I hope you'll see my movies—again, and again, and again. I hope you'll be my friend and my fan. I'd love for you to be my lover, I know you would treat me well, and I would surely treat you VERY WELL—you can see the promise in my eyes, can't you? My promise is Romance, not sex—anyway, not just sex! I am Romance, the emblem of the revolutionary new Romantic-Sexual world of *Playboy,* so shocking (and so exciting!) in 1953, and soon to triumph in the liberated sixties. Both Marilyn Monroe and *Playboy* would soar to unprecedented heights of fame and fortune—and notoriety! We were heralds of the new era, years before our time. We were the very spirit of the new freedom and there was never anything vicious or dark or cruel or mean-spirited about us. Of course, we were misjudged by many. We were publicly reviled, and admired; we were denounced, and envied, and emulated—that's our revenge. Shouldn't I be proud? America's #1 Dream Girl! The Sweetheart of America's unconscious! Romance—the promise of sex as it should be! As famous, I predict, in the 21st century as I'd been in the second half of the 20th! And why?—because, as you can see, I promise fun, laughs, a good time—nothing "neurotic" or "tragic." My secret is, all I ever wanted was to please you—and you, and *you.* I grew up in an orphanage and foster homes in the Los Angeles area, so I've always been desperate to please others—so I'd be loved. I was terrified of being alone, and if you're not loved you will be alone, and how can you be loved except to please people— again, and again, and again? In Hollywood, it was decided early on in my career that I was a tramp. I'd make money for the industry, but I was cheap, low-life, I was "promiscuous" and the Establishment felt smug detesting me. Look how I dressed!—or *un*dressed! Look at the sensational publicity I received, everywhere I went! In my early prime I was already bringing into the studio $25 million a year—and paid $50,000. I'd say that was a good deal for Hollywood, wouldn't you? Still, they didn't respect me. They didn't like me. I wasn't one of "their own"—like Elizabeth Taylor. Sure, I took my revenge on them in my later career—hours late on the set, or wouldn't show up at all, forever sick—always a "virus" or a "fever"—costing them millions of dollars in production costs they wouldn't spend on *me*—can you blame me? And what did I do wrong? Isn't a woman supposed to be an object of desire? an object of longing? of pleasure, if only in fantasy? It was MARILYN MONROE fans adored—why couldn't you all respect me, too? Was that too much to ask? Look how I'm smiling—you'd almost guess I could foresee my fame, you'd never guess how anxious I was, yes and suicidal even at 23. How many nude photos of pretty young girls have been taken in America, and how many have survived beyond even a single appearance in print? How many "starlets"—even "stars"? Shouldn't I be grateful for whatever I had? Maybe I was exploited— but what was the alternative?

What would have been my fate, if not this? So I'm not bitter. Really, I'm not! All I hope from you is you'll gaze upon me with love, maybe with tenderness and longing, I wouldn't even ask for respect. My very name MARI-LYN MONROE was not my own, it was chosen for me by studio bosses—but it's become one of the great names of history. What a joke on *them!* When I died, MARI-LYN MONROE appeared in front-page headlines around the world. What a loss! What a tragic irony— MARILYN MONROE who's so beautiful, famous— only 36 years old—on August 5, 1962—they'd claim that I died of a massive barbiturate overdose and that I'd com-mitted suicide— but it wasn't that way, at all. It's just I was feeling so melancholy for months, for years, for my lifetime maybe. My first husband I'd loved so much had left me, my mother had left me to be raised in an orphan-age and foster homes, my father would never acknowl-edge my very existence, my marriages failed because I needed so much more than any man could provide. My last lover was a famous man, I won't say his name because it is a name I revere, he too would die within a few years, of an assassin's bullet, I was in love with him or believed I was and he was a married man, a family man, when he tried to break with me I became hysterical, I behaved badly I suppose, I called him, threatened to expose him, I didn't mean it, but—you know how women are! How desperate women are. In the night I was alone, I took sleeping pills and lost count of how many I'd taken, this had happened to me before, "suicide attempts" they were called but I refuse to think that I was suicidal, or that I died by design. My life as Norma Jeane was an accidental life, from the first—why would I die by my own hand? Some even claim that MARILYN MONROE might have been murdered—but that isn't true, either. MARILYN MONROE just—ended. She was a fantasy balloon blown up bigger and bigger and finally beyond all human proportion and even comprehension and the girl you see here, MISS GOLDEN DREAMS, was smothered inside, and at last—ended. But I *am* smiling, see? In my heart, I'm happy. I'm the girl-next-door who refuses to dwell upon morbidity—that's not the American way. I'm a beautiful girl but I'm pretty, too—my beauty isn't classical or ethereal or mystical, like the *Mona Lisa*—my beauty is down-to-earth, sensuous, natural. So let's be happy together, please! Remember me like this, age 23, *Playboy's* premiere centerfold, as luscious in the new century as in the old! Just you and me. Tell me what you like best, and I'll do it. I'll keep every secret of yours, I promise. Only just love me. And think of me sometime.

Promise?

Love,

Marilyn

# some like her hot:
## marilyn and sex

*I*t's virtually impossible to talk about Monroe's sexual appeal without sounding a little feeble-minded: any attempt to describe her particular erotic sheen can hardly refrain from restating the obvious, like calling the sky blue or the sun hot. Yet the effect her abundant sexuality had on those who were exposed to it still manages to bear its own distinctive stamp.

In Alice Elliott Dark's "Too Sexy, Sexy Too," the author offers a wistful, backward glance at her girlhood, and the way Monroe's sexual shimmer seemed to point to and illuminate the mysteries of her own burgeoning sexuality. Dark, a fiction writer whose haunting story "In the Gloaming" was adapted for film by HBO and Trinity Playhouse, uses her wry and deft intelligence to recall Monroe's effect on the youngest of her female viewers.

Poet and critic Albert Mobilio offers the other side of the equation: Marilyn's effect on men. By examining Billy Wilder's *The Seven Year Itch* from the male—in this case Tom Ewell's—point of view, Mobilio establishes a connection between the hapless protagonist and the vast male audience who sat quietly in the darkened theater wishing, just wishing, that they were in Ewell's shoes.

# TOO SEXY, SEXY TOO
*Alice Elliott Dark*

*S*he was there, a breeze, a vapor weaving through the summer evenings while we ran after fireflies. Marilyn. Marilyn.

In those days, suburban parents went to parties without their children and we saw what they were like when they left us, how differently they dressed to be with other grown-ups, the perfume and the aftershave, the high heels. Sometimes we saw how they were when they came back, swaying from side to side. Tipsy. A clear doctor's-office smell arrived with their midnight kisses.

48    We didn't care much what they did while they were
gone, but when they came back—weren't they ours,
then?

No, they were not.

They drifted into our bedrooms for a moment, their
clothes swishing, their scents enveloping, and then they
were off down the hall. Why not stay with us, sitting on
our beds, hearing about our evenings, the baby-sitter, the
fights? What was more interesting?

SHE WAS THE star then. My mother didn't like her.
Too blond. As far as sexpots went, my mother preferred
Ava Gardner.

We didn't see Marilyn much—posters outside the
movie theater, pictures in magazines. We tried to figure
out why they talked about her, why they winked and
raised their eyebrows, but we didn't get it. She wore a
lot of makeup; was it that? White hair; that was childlike, wasn't it? We didn't know exactly. We were undis-
cerning when it came to her appeal. We saw the smile
but not, yet, the shame.

THE MEN LIKED that she married a baseball player.

WE DIDN'T KNOW much. We didn't wonder much,
either, or ask too many questions. We were children, and

knew it. When sex broke into our world—and it did, of course—we watched it as if we were Eve drawing close to hear the message of the snake. The facts made it sound disgusting, but what about how it felt to have the ocean pound against our bodies, or the comfort we got from sitting with our heels pressed in the hollow between our legs? What about what it was like to discover chiffon and the way it slipped across our skin? Or the sensation of strawberry juice dribbling down our chests. The longing to climb higher and higher into a thrusting tree. The inkling that there was something out there for us, something that would make us wild and giddy and nuts and willing. The sense that we could open up, and that the opening would be deep, endlessly deep. That we were more than our parts, more yet than the sum of them, even as we were also our strong, vigorous bodies. We weren't inside and outside, but one. Girls. Souls incarnate. Our childhoods were sensual and thoughtful. We were waiting to be ourselves, all of a piece.

PIN UP. ARMS up. Breasts up. The white dress, blowing up. That breathy "Mr. President."

AND THEN IT was over. We snuck a look at the pictures in *Life* magazine and heard words from the adult world—misery, suicide, drugs, affairs. Peter Lawford. Bobby Kennedy. Jack—Mr. President. The names swirled beyond us, above our heads. We were kept from the truth, protected, but it breezed around us anyway. She was dead, naked, on a bed with silky sheets. Out in California, where the movie stars lived, she was dead. It was sad, tragic even, but also not so surprising, considering. We understood that there was something about her that was destined for such an end. We got that she was too sexy, and that she'd died because of it.

Somehow.

SHE WAS DEAD.

Our lives went on. We didn't think about her much, not directly at least, but she was there, the image, the influence, the female, the sexiest of all. We wanted to be sexy, too, but not like that. Not a victim! Yet what else was there? Was there life beyond breasts and snickering? At camp, we huddled together before the Sunday morning naked bath in the lake and wished we were still flat. Boys, brothers, snapped our bras and pinched us. A counselor told us that masturbating was when two boys rubbed asses. We tried, but nothing happened. How could boys enjoy that? They were weird, for sure. But they were also cute, especially their forearms and their shoulders and their jawlines. When the time came, we kissed them, in spite of our differences. And it felt, for the most part, very nice.

———

## NORMA JEANE BAKER.

We saw her movies later. The first, for me, was *Gentlemen Prefer Blondes.* I found the title discouraging, but the movie wasn't. It was funny. She was funny. No one had said that, ever, when they talked about her. She was funny and bright and sweet and no one had ever said.

How could people snicker at a girl who was so complete? What did a girl have to do to be a person?

She was pretty, too, in her little suits with fur at her neck.

We looked at each other, wondering.


## LEGEND.

Suddenly, somehow, we are the ones going out on July evenings, but dressed casually, and usually with our children. We sit on each others' patios and joke about our sex lives, hinting that they're virtually nonexistent. Who can have sex with kids around?

The kids, though, are up to something. They dress as they've learned from the mags, and it's all sexy. They pierce and tattoo and color and can balance on extraordinarily high shoes. Official letters come home from the junior highs, informing us of an epidemic of casual oral sex at preteen parties. It seems they've been led to believe it's safer than intercourse and, according to their Mr. President, it's not even real sex.

At least it's mutual, my husband points out.

*all the available light*

It's nothing, the kids shrug. Everyone does it. It feels good.

Yes, we say, but . . .

But what? Some of us are appalled that they're having sex so young. I think it's preferable to the opposite, the centuries of ignorance and repression. And anyway, a lot of us had sex young, too. We came to sex in the sixties and seventies, when it was there for the asking. Like our children, we didn't have to wait until we got home with our husbands, didn't have to do it in the context of marriage and behind closed doors. We didn't need perfume, or even much grooming; unlike our mothers, some of us left our body hair intact. We didn't accept that sex was dirty and bad, and fought the notion within ourselves until we felt clean and fine, no matter what. We were sexy, but we demanded to be individuals, too.

I don't think Marilyn had that luxury. So much of what she was was what the world thought of her.

We are in her debt for the price she paid for her sexiness. We took what she offered and ran with it. We gave our children their freedom.

But where are our summer nights?

## SCRATCHING TOM EWELL'S ITCH

*Albert Mobilio*

His thumb twitches. His neck is in spasm. He paces. He skulks. He chain-smokes as if cigarettes are mother's milk. His crimped, squirrelly face winces at her approach since she might, with a judicious swing of her ample hip, knock him sprawling on the floor. Like Hamlet, he pleads his quandary of conscience, rehearsing absolutions and penances, yet he's the Dane with a flaming crotch, a man taking arms against a sea of woman troubles. He's a Freudian case study of an extreme state of repression.

This "happily married man" is Tom Ewell, and Marilyn Monroe has moved in upstairs and she's cooling her underpants in the icebox, claims to "drink like a fish," and thinks he's just so "delicate."

What's a guy to do? What does the red-blooded American male do when the world's greatest cock-teaser selects his humble member to tease? That, of course, is the prickling question behind Billy Wilder's 1955 comedy *The Seven Year Itch*. The movie's slender plot—average Joe tempted by sex goddess—is hardly complicated by anything as heady as character development or psychological depth. Indeed, the cartoon quality of Ewell's harried husband and Monroe's blithely potent Dazzledent Toothpaste Girl heightens the mythic overtones of the tale. Think of Actaeon spying on Diana or Odysseus lashed to the mast while the Sirens drive him mad with lust. In such stark tales, the cost of desire is weighed with fierce precision. The movie, too, is cautionary, constituting a warning to 1950s work-a-daddies not to stray. (The 1980s would produce a bloodier version of this morality play—*Fatal Attraction*—that the Greeks would have surely loved.)

Ewell stumbles into Monroe's blond orbit, trembles mightily, and then barely escapes intact. She not only renders him tongue-tied but sets his whole body shuddering so that in many scenes he appears on the brink of some awful detonation. What else could we expect of this middle-management pencil-chewer? Ewell's character, Richard Sherman, works at a paperback publisher where he dreams up lascivious covers for editions of *Little Women;* something of a Walter Mitty type, he believes he possesses "an animal thing" when it comes to women. But after he puts his wife and son on a train out of town, her maternal voice remains to haunt him: as he's about to pry the cap off a bottle of health drink (-she's warned him away from alcohol) using the cabinet knob, he hears her imperious command to use the opener. Seemingly born henpecked, he's the slightly naughty boy in a grown-up's body, a very married variant on the hapless Everyman played by actors like Jack Lemmon or Bob Cummings.

Even though Ewell promises there will be no smoking or drinking while the wife is gone (and she'll be calling every night at ten just to check), within minutes of Monroe's appearance in his apartment he is, of course, resorting to those vices and plotting even more. The married stiff who's been sipping health drink with a grimace transforms almost instantly into a jittery Casanova who, in his wildly percolating imagination, seduces his giddy neighbor by playing Rachmaninoff and announcing, "Now I'm going to take you in my arms and kiss you very quickly and very hard." His fantasy of suave Continental manners lends little to his actual lovemaking technique: in a flailing attempt to kiss Monroe "very hard," the two end up falling on the floor in a tangle of limbs and apologies. "Nothing like this ever happened to me

*all the available light*

before in my life," he stammers. "Honest? It happens to me all the time," she airily replies.

Ewell captures the predicament of the sexually tormented man in acutely deployed body language that reveals confident and craven to be different sides of the same emotional coin. His eyes can go in an instant from wide-eyed expectation to darting slivers. His hands and legs seem controlled by an apoplectic puppeteer: Ewell wants to be a smooth operator but the mind-body tumult Monroe instigates is uncontainable. When he gets close to her his movements speed up jerkily; he's so agitated he can't pour her champagne without overflowing the brim. The sexual metaphor is given an even more submissive twist as Ewell himself sips off the excess from her dribbling glass. The emasculated "nice guy," Ewell not only can't control his glee in the presence of a sex goddess but he's more than willing to clean up afterward.

What you see of the famous skirt scene where Monroe stands above a subway grate and coos with delight as a blast of air billows her dress was mostly filmed on a sound stage in Hollywood. Little more than Marilyn's knees are visible in a quick cut below her waist. But, on location in New York, she repeatedly allowed the dress to rise up above her hips, revealing a nearly diaphanous pair of white panties to thousands of Lexington Avenue bystanders and amateur photographers, including her then husband DiMaggio. (Later that night, crew members at the hotel where the couple stayed heard fighting.

The next day she had bruises.) Censors cut what was perhaps the most apt line from the scene. As the subway blows air up her skirt, Marilyn asks Ewell, "Don't you wish you could wear skirts? I feel so sorry for you men in your hot pants." Ewell's certainly are. In the scene, he cadges a kiss from Monroe by inquiring if, as she claims in her toothpaste commercial, the product really leaves one's mouth "kissing sweet." What man hasn't connived like this for sex, experiencing the thrill of attainment rapidly undercut by the humiliating taint of being a sneak. To steal a kiss is to take something undeserved, to obtain it by wiles, or more precisely, feminine wiles. Indeed, the only way for Ewell to get some relief from those hot trousers is, as Monroe says, to wear a skirt.

The year after *Itch,* Ewell played the same role with Jayne Mansfield in *The Girl Can't Help It.* Once again, it was homo erectus versus sex bomb. Both films are chock-full of double-entendres and sly visual puns that reflect the growing mass awareness of psychoanalytic thought in the 1950s. There's Mansfield clutching two bottles of milk in front of her chest, or Monroe asking Ewell about a bottle of champagne, "Do you think you could get it open?" "It's simply a matter of pressure and counterpressure," he blusters. Functioning as a shrink-savvy gloss to *Itch*'s shenanigans is a chapter in a manuscript Ewell is reading entitled "The Repressed Urge in the Middle-Aged Male." It details the clinical condition of the "seven-year itch," an affliction of lust striking

*all the available light*

otherwise contentedly married men. Ewell confesses to the appropriately European-accented analyst who wrote the book: "Doctor, I'm in serious trouble. I'm married." Marriage is an ailment and Ewell its suffering victim. When Monroe spies his wedding ring, she asks if he has any children. "No," he stammers, desperately trying to deny the severity of his illness. "Well, just one. Little. Very little. Hardly counts." Keeping faithful in the face of Monroe's temptation worries him sick. In a moment of guilty self-castigation, he looks in a mirror to see his face grow haggard, his hair stand on end. The "repressed urge" is poisoning him from the inside out; Tom Ewell is a martyr to marital fidelity.

At the end of the film, with Ewell's monogamy preserved, Monroe rhapsodizes about how Ewell, the Milquetoast hubby, is exactly "what pretty girls want," a "nice guy" who's "off in the corner nervous and shy." It's a consoling message for Ewell as well as those besotted male moviegoers who've been watching her with slack-jawed admiration. Yet off-screen, Monroe's husbands and lovers were hardly shrinking violets—Joseph Schenck, Alfred Kazin, Arthur Miller, Joe DiMaggio, and Jack Kennedy typify the kind of top-dog alpha males Monroe would never fall for in the movies. These were men who hit her or used her (as she used them) in an arena governed by male power; Marilyn could never have played a role in which such realpolitik sexual bargains were struck. Her most successful screen companions were feminized schemers like Ewell and Tony Curtis. Even the macho Frenchman Yves Montand put on a figurative dress to get a peek up Marilyn's. In *Let's Make Love,* he played a billionaire who becomes a song-and-dance man in order to get close to struggling actress Monroe. If, in movies, she had dallied with men who "strut around like tigers," as she describes them to Ewell, it would have spoiled the fantasy that she was attainable for all of us nervous Nellies off in our corners. (Not to mention sharpening the jealous disdain many women already felt toward her.)

Ewell proved to be Marilyn's ideal screen lover. Conflicted, agitated, and ultimately unfulfilled, he is the man nobody wants to be or wants to marry but, in fact, is the man most men are and most women marry. His two evenings with Marilyn constitute his glancing tryst with something epic: a woman who is less a person than a state of being. Indeed, Monroe is billed in the credits as simply The Girl—an archetype of pure urge. And by repressing his own desire, Ewell sacrifices his sexual satisfaction so that the rest of the male tribe can thumb-suck upon this reassurance: it's not that Marilyn Monroe (or someone like her) doesn't want you; it's because you, being such a "nice guy," don't really want her. Tom Ewell itched (but didn't scratch) for the uncommitted sins of naughty little men everywhere.

# boot in the face:
## monroe as victim

It can be argued that off the screen Monroe had a more vivid and varied existence than she did on; her short, eventful life has been recast again and again, sometimes as a story of triumph, others as one of defeat. Of the many feminists who have written about her, both Gloria Steinem in the 1980s and Kate Millett in the 1990s subscribe to the belief of Monroe as victim, most significantly of the patriarchy that was Hollywood and indeed the world. The selection reprinted here is from Steinem's powerful 1986 book on Monroe, while Millett's short, biting piece was first published in the catalog of a traveling exhibition entitled "Elvis + Marilyn: 2X Immortal," which featured paintings, collages, sculpture, and other visual images of the two stars.

In contrast to these two relatively recent pieces, the article written by Clare Boothe Luce, "The 'Love Goddess' Who Never Found Any Love," was the cover story for the August 7, 1964, issue of *Life* magazine, appearing just two years after Monroe's death. Luce, a well-regarded playwright (her acid-tongued play *The Women* was famously adapted for the screen) and journalist, adopts a tone that is both more gentle and elegiac than that of Steinem and Millett. Still, her underlying belief in Monroe's victimhood is essentially the same, though she points to Monroe's skewed and anguished childhood as the real oppressor.

Finally, Marge Piercy's "Looking Good" discerns a political subtext in Monroe's life. Piercy, a novelist and poet whose sustained political commitment and activism have shaped her own extensive output, claims that while Monroe may have indeed had political views, it is hard to imagine her engaged in any kind of overt political activity. The eternal sex kitten played by Monroe was not a political being of any kind; she wielded no power, she commanded no respect. And according to Piercy, it was respect—for which Monroe longed but was never given—that just may have saved her.

*I knew I belonged to the public and to the world, not because I was talented or even beautiful but because I had never belonged to anything or anyone else.* —FROM THE UNFINISHED AUTOBIOGRAPHY OF MARILYN MONROE

## THE WOMAN WHO WILL NOT DIE
*Gloria Steinem*

*I*t has been nearly a quarter of a century since the death of a minor American actress named Marilyn Monroe. There is no reason for her to be part of my consciousness as I walk down a midtown New York street filled with color and action and life.

In a shopwindow display of white summer dresses, I see several huge photographs—a life-size cutout of Marilyn standing in a white halter dress, some close-ups of her vulnerable, please-love-me smile—but they don't look dated. Oddly, Marilyn seems to be just as much a part of this street scene as the neighboring images of models who could now be her daughters—even her granddaughters.

I walk another block and pass a record store featuring the hit albums of a rock star named Madonna. She has imitated Marilyn Monroe's hair, style, and clothes, but subtracted her vulnerability. Instead of using seduction to offer men whatever they want, Madonna uses it to get what she wants—a 1980s difference that has made her the idol of teenage girls. Nevertheless, her international symbols of femaleness are pure Marilyn.

A few doors away, a bookstore displays two volumes on Marilyn Monroe in its well-stocked window. The first is nothing but random photographs, one of many such collections that have been published over the years. The second is one of several recent exposés on the circumstances surrounding Monroe's 1962 death from an accidental or purposeful overdose of sleeping pills. Could organized crime, Jimmy Hoffa in particular, have planned to use her friendship with the Kennedys and her suicide—could Hoffa or his friends even have caused that suicide—in order to embarrass or blackmail Robert Kennedy, who was definitely a Mafia enemy and probably her lover? Only a few months ago, Marilyn Monroe's name made international headlines again when a British television documentary on this conspiracy theory was shown and a network documentary made in the United States was suppressed, with potential pressure from crime-controlled unions or from the late Robert Kennedy's family as rumored reasons.

As I turn the corner into my neighborhood, I pass a newsstand where the face of one more young Marilyn Monroe look-alike stares up at me from a glossy magazine cover. She is Kate Mailer, Norman Mailer's daughter, who was born the year that Marilyn Monroe died. Now she is starring in *Strawhead,* a "memory play" about Monroe written by Norman Mailer, who is so obsessed with this long-dead sex goddess that he had written one long biography and another work—half fact, half fiction—about her, even before casting his daughter in this part.

The next morning, I turn on the television and see a promotion for a show on film director Billy Wilder. The only clip chosen to attract viewers and represent Wilder's entire career is one of Marilyn Monroe singing a few breathless bars in *Some Like It Hot,* one of two films they made together.

These are everyday signs of a unique longevity. If you add her years of movie stardom to the years since her death, Marilyn Monroe has been part of our lives and imaginations for nearly four decades. That's a very long time for one celebrity to survive in a throwaway culture.

In the 1930s, when English critic Cyril Connolly proposed a definition of posterity to measure whether a writer's work had stood the test of time, he suggested that posterity should be limited to ten years. The form

*all the available light*

and content of popular culture were changing too fast, he explained, to make any artist accountable for more than a decade.

Since then, the pace of change has been accelerated even more. Everything from the communications revolution to multinational entertainment has altered the form of culture. Its content has been transformed by civil rights, feminism, an end to film censorship, and much more. Nonetheless, Monroe's personal and intimate ability to inhabit our fantasies has gone right on. As I write this, she is still better known than most living movie stars, most world leaders, and most television personalities. The surprise is that she rarely has been taken seriously enough to ask why that is so.

One simple reason for her life story's endurance is the premature end of it. Personalities and narratives projected onto the screen of our imaginations are far more haunting—and far more likely to be the stuff of conspiracies and conjecture—if they have not been allowed to play themselves out to their logical or illogical ends. James Dean's brief life is the subject of a cult, but the completed lives of such similar "outsiders" as Gary Cooper or Henry Fonda are not. Each day in the brief Camelot of John Kennedy inspires as much speculation as each year in the long New Deal of Franklin Roosevelt. The few years of Charlie "Bird" Parker's music inspire graffiti ("Bird Lives"), but the many musical years of Duke Ellington do not.

When the past dies, there is mourning, but when the future dies, our imaginations are compelled to carry it on.

Would Marilyn Monroe have become the serious actress she aspired to be? Could she have survived the transition from sex goddess to mortal woman that aging would impose? Could she have stopped her disastrous marriages to men whose images she wanted to absorb (Beloved American DiMaggio, Serious Intellectual Miller), and found a partner who loved and understood her as she really was? Could she have kicked her life-wasting habits of addiction and procrastination? Would she have had or adopted children? Found support in the growing strength of women or been threatened by it? Entered the world of learning or continued to be ridiculed for trying? Survived and even enjoyed the age of sixty she now would be?

Most important, could she finally have escaped her lifetime combination of two parts talent, one part victim, and one part joke? Would she have been "taken seriously," as she so badly wanted to be?

We will never know. Every question is as haunting as any of its possible answers.

But the poignancy of this incompleteness is not enough to explain Marilyn Monroe's enduring power. Even among brief public lives, few become parables. Those that endure seem to hook into our deepest emotions of hope or fear, dream or nightmare, of what our own fates might be. Successful leaders also fall into one group or the other: those who invoke a threatening future and promise disaster unless we obey, and those who conjure up a hopeful future and promise reward if we will follow. It's this power of either fear or hope that makes a personal legend survive, from the fearsome extreme of Adolf Hitler (Did he really escape? Might he have lived on in the jungles of South America?) to the hopeful myth of Zapata waiting in the hills of Mexico to rescue his people. The same is true for the enduring fictions of popular culture, from the frightening villain to the hopeful hero, each of whom is reincarnated again and again.

In an intimate way during her brief life, Marilyn Monroe hooked into both those extremes of emotion. She personified many of the secret hopes of men and many secret fears of women.

To men, wrote Norman Mailer, her image was "gorgeous, forgiving, humorous, compliant and tender . . . she would ask no price." She was the child-woman who offered pleasure without adult challenge; a lover who neither judged nor asked anything in return. Both the roles she played and her own public image embodied a masculine hope for a woman who is innocent and sensuously experienced at the same time. "In fact," as Marilyn said toward the end of her career, "my popularity seemed almost entirely a masculine phenomenon."

Since most men have experienced female power only in their childhoods, they associate it with a time when they themselves were powerless. This will continue as long as children are raised almost totally by women, and rarely see women in authority outside the home. That's why male adults, and some females too, experience the presence of a strong woman as a dangerous regression to a time of their own vulnerability and dependence. For men, especially, who are trained to measure manhood and maturity by their distance from the world of women, being forced back to that world for female companionship may be very threatening indeed. A compliant child-woman like Monroe solves this dilemma by offering sex *without* the power of an adult woman, much less of an equal. As a child herself, she allows men to feel both conquering and protective; to be both dominating and admirable at the same time.

For women, Monroe embodied kinds of fear that were just as basic as the hope she offered men: the fear of a sexual competitor who could take away men on whom women's identities and even livelihoods might depend; the fear of having to meet her impossible standard of always giving—and asking nothing in return; the nagging fear that we might share her feminine fate of being vulnerable, unserious, constantly in danger of becoming a victim.

Aside from her beautiful face, which women envied, she was nothing like the female stars that women moviegoers have made popular. Those stars offered at least the illusion of being in control of their fates—and perhaps having an effect on the world. Stars of the classic "women's movies" were actresses like Bette Davis, who made her impact by sheer force of emotion; or Katharine Hepburn, who was always intelligent and never victimized for long; or even Doris Day, who charmed the world into conforming to her own virginal standards. Their figures were admirable and neat, but without the vulnerability of the big-breasted woman in a society that regresses men and keeps them obsessed with the maternal symbols of breasts and hips.

Watching Monroe was quite different: women were forced to worry about her vulnerability—and thus their own. They might feel like a black moviegoer watching a black actor play a role that was too passive, too obedient, or a Jew watching a Jewish character who was selfish and avaricious. In spite of some extra magic, some face-saving sincerity and humor, Marilyn Monroe was still close to the humiliating stereotype of a dumb blonde: depersonalized, sexual, even a joke. Though few women yet had the self-respect to object on behalf of their sex, as one would object on behalf of a race or religion, they still might be left feeling a little humiliated—or threatened—without knowing why.

"I have always had a talent for irritating women since I was fourteen," Marilyn wrote in her unfinished autobiography. "Sometimes I've been to a party where no one spoke to me for a whole evening. The men, frightened by their wives or sweeties, would give me a wide berth. And the ladies would gang up in a corner to discuss my dangerous character."

But all that was before her death and the revelations surrounding it. The moment she was gone, Monroe's vulnerability was no longer just a turn-on for many men and an embarrassment for many women. It was a tragedy. Whether that final overdose was suicide or not, both men and women were forced to recognize the insecurity and private terrors that had caused her to attempt suicide several times before.

Men who had never known her wondered if their love and protection might have saved her. Women who had never known her wondered if their empathy and friendship might have done the same. For both women and men, the ghost of Marilyn came to embody a particularly powerful form of hope: the rescue fantasy. Not only did we imagine a happier ending for the parable of Marilyn Monroe's life, but we also fantasized ourselves as the saviors who could have brought it about.

Still, women didn't seem quite as comfortable about going public with their rescue fantasies as men did. It meant admitting an identity with a woman who always had been a little embarrassing, and who had now turned out to be doomed as well. Nearly all of the journalistic eulogies that followed Monroe's death were written by men. So are almost all of the more than forty books that have been published about Monroe.

Bias in the minds of editors played a role, too. Consciously or not, they seemed to assume that only male journalists should write about a sex goddess. Margaret Parton, a reporter for the *Ladies' Home Journal* and one of the few women assigned to profile Marilyn during her lifetime, wrote an article that was rejected because it was too favorable. She had reported Marilyn's ambitious hope of playing Sadie Thompson, under the guidance of Lee Strasberg, in a television version of *Rain,* based on a short story by Somerset Maugham. (Sadie Thompson was "a girl who knew how to be gay, even when she was sad," a fragile Marilyn had explained, "and that's important—you know?") Parton also reported her own "sense of having met a sick little canary instead of a peacock. Only when you pick it up in your hand to comfort it . . . beneath the sickness, the weakness and the innocence, you find a strong bone structure, and a heart beating. You *recognize* sickness, and you *find* strength."

Bruce and Beatrice Gould, editors of the *Ladies' Home Journal,* told Parton she must have been "mesmerized" to write something so uncritical. "If you were a man," Mr. Gould told her, "I'd wonder what went on that afternoon in Marilyn's apartment." Fred Guiles, one of Marilyn Monroe's more fair-minded biographers, counted the suppression of this sensitive article as one proof that many editors were interested in portraying Monroe, at least in those later years, as "crazy, a home wrecker."

Just after Monroe's death, one of the few women to write with empathy was Diana Trilling, an author confident enough not to worry about being trivialized by association—and respected enough to get published. Trilling regretted the public's "mockery of [Marilyn's] wish to be educated," and her dependence on sexual artifice that must have left "a great emptiness where a true sexuality would have supplied her with a sense of herself as a person." She mourned Marilyn's lack of friends, "especially women, to whose protectiveness her extreme vulnerability spoke so directly."

"But we were the friends," as Trilling said sadly, "of whom she knew nothing."

In fact, the contagion of feminism that followed Monroe's death by less than a decade may be the newest and most powerful reason for the continuing strength of her legend. As women began to be honest in public, and to discover that many of our experiences were more societal than individual, we also realized that we could benefit more by acting together than by deserting each other. We were less likely to blame or be the victim, whether Marilyn or ourselves, and more likely to rescue ourselves and each other.

In 1972, the tenth anniversary of her death and the birth year of *Ms.*, the first magazine to be published by and for women, Harriet Lyons, one of its early editors, suggested that *Ms.* do a cover story about Marilyn called "The Woman Who Died Too Soon." As the writer of this brief essay about women's new hope of reclaiming Marilyn, I was astounded by the response to the article. It was like tapping an underground river of interest. For instance:

*all the available light*

Marilyn had talked about being sexually assaulted as a child, though many of her biographers had not believed her. Women wrote in to tell their similar stories. It was my first intimation of what since has become a documented statistic: one in six adult women has been sexually assaulted in childhood by a family member. The long-lasting effects—for instance, feeling one has no value except a sexual one—seemed shared by these women and by Marilyn. Yet most were made to feel guilty and alone, and many were as disbelieved by the grown-ups around them as Marilyn had been.

Physicians had been more likely to prescribe sleeping pills and tranquilizers than to look for the cause of Monroe's sleeplessness and anxiety. They had continued to do so even after she had attempted suicide several times. Women responded with their own stories of being over-medicated, and of doctors who assumed women's physical symptoms were "all in their minds." It was my first understanding that women are more likely to be given chemical and other arm's-length treatment, and to suffer from the assumption that they can be chemically calmed or sedated with less penalty because they are doing only "women's work." Then, ads in medical journals blatantly recommended tranquilizers for depressed housewives, and even now the majority of all tranquilizer prescriptions are written for women.

Acting, modeling, making a living more from external appearance than from internal identity—these had been Marilyn's lifelines out of poverty and obscurity.

Other women who had suppressed their internal selves to become interchangeable "pretty girls"—and as a result were struggling with both lack of identity and terror of aging—wrote to tell their stories.

To gain the seriousness and respect that was largely denied her, and to gain the fatherly protection she had been completely denied, Marilyn married a beloved American folk hero and then a respected intellectual. Other women who had tried to marry for protection or for identity, as women often are encouraged to do, wrote to say how impossible and childlike this had been for them, and how impossible for the husbands who were expected to provide their wives' identities. But Marilyn did not live long enough to see a time in which women sought their own identities, not just derived ones.

During her marriage to Arthur Miller, Marilyn had tried to have a child—but suffered an ectopic pregnancy, a miscarriage—and could not. Letters poured in from women who also suffered from this inability and from a definition of womanhood so tied to the accident of the physical ability to bear a child—preferably a son, as Marilyn often said, though later she also talked of a daughter—that their whole sense of self had been undermined. "Manhood means many things," as one reader explained, "but womanhood means only one." And where is the self-respect of a woman who wants to give birth only to a male child, someone different from herself?

Most of all, women readers mourned that Marilyn had lived and died in an era when there were so few ways for her to know that these experiences were shared with other women, that she was not alone.

Now women and men bring the past quarter century of change and understanding to these poignant photographs taken in the days just before her death. It makes them all the more haunting. [Editor's Note: This chapter originally appeared with photographs, which are not represented here.]

I still see the self-consciousness with which she posed for a camera. It makes me remember my own teenage discomfort at seeing her on the screen, mincing and whispering and simply hoping her way into love and approval. By holding a mirror to the exaggerated ways in which female human beings are trained to act, she could be as embarrassing—and as sad and revealing—as a female impersonator.

Yet now I also see the why of it, and the woman behind the mask that her self-consciousness creates.

I still feel worried about her, just as I did then. There is something especially vulnerable about big-breasted women in this world concerned with such bodies, but unconcerned with the real person within. We may envy these women a little, yet we feel protective of them, too.

But in these photographs, the body emphasis seems more the habit of some former self. It's her face we look at. Now that we know the end of her story, it's the real woman we hope to find—looking out of the eyes of Marilyn.

In the last interview before her death, close to the time of these photographs, Patricia Newcomb, her friend and press secretary, remembers that Marilyn pleaded unsuccessfully with the reporter to end his article like this:

What I really want to say: That what the world really needs is a real feeling of kinship. Everybody: stars, laborers, Negroes, Jews, Arabs. We are all brothers.

Please don't make me a joke. End the interview with what I believe.

## MARILYN, WE HARDLY KNEW YOU
*Kate Millett*

*I*t wasn't till they killed her that they understood.
Up to that point, they were perfectly content
with their bimbo, their pinup, their dumb blonde. That
she aspired in her art, that she was a brilliant comedienne, that she knelt before Lee Strasberg and left him
half her estate in homage, never entered the picture.
Marilyn was meat. Till she was dead meat. The most
significant element in her death was that she died naked.
That's how they saw her. The whole bunch of them,
even the women. I, too—an adolescent at the moment

of her death and for that instant at one with my culture. One gasped . . . naked. One imagined—no, one *saw* the corpse. Dressed only in that magnificent skin. Gradually, the voyeurs relented—but it took a while. Hadn't they made her a slut, sacrificed her to the locker-room door, subsumed her into a collective masturbatory fantasy? The generic whore of an entire generation of men on earth.

One looked on as a woman—or rather a woman in the making—and admired her beauty, scarcely perceived her art or humor, but burned with shame. As she was cheapened, so were we all—was she not the most perfect among us? That her grandeur could be tits and ass, that her innocent good will could be derided not only by lechery but by cleverness: for they made her represent stupidity as well as gorgeous breasts. Female inferiority incorporated in female flesh. So that masculine ambition could assume intellectual superiority even as it sated itself, able in one gesture to ravish and disdain. The very stratagem that created the dumb blonde, the bimbo. How much more accommodating than earlier Jezebels who exercised real power within their sin—the bimbo is so stupid, so contemptible, one is scarcely aware of the power of her carnality. It is defused, turned to plastic. Styrofoam, a commodity mere paper, the centerfold: at the extreme edge mankind fucks a great inflated rubber doll—harmless.

As to the living woman—she is only marginally hu-

*all the available light*

man because so negligible intellectually—the exploitation of her flesh is but another way to humiliate and lord it over her, cheat or expropriate her. A shell game: deceit rendering the effort of assault unnecessary. You talked her into it—she was willing—she was even hot. She giggled. You stuck it to her and she ate it up. When it's over, you remember that. That she was willing. Disgusted with the knee-jerk automatic disgust of lust, the puritan acts fast to punish the very assent he had manufactured. Heaping on her further humiliation by giving her the name of whore. She will be the more possessed through this word, belong more utterly to her masters. Best of all, it will isolate her from the women. There will be no succor from her own kind.

So she was used. Nearly used up. Growing shaky by the end. Marilyn was getting fired from pictures. Martin Luther King, Jr., was at the nadir of his career when someone shot him into eternity. Marilyn was failing to show up sometimes, breaking finally, hardly able to keep going. And then a hand raised against her. Her own or another's—for the observer at the time there was no difference. The most remarkable detail of her death was its nudity. We never suspected foul play: suicide was the appropriate thing, the end of the gangbang, as murder of one kind or another is the logical outcome of pornography. She'd "do herself in." The scapegoat itself executing the general sentence. It was the predicted act, the expected thing, the inevitable sacrificial denouement.

Didn't Janis overdose? Didn't Anne Sexton turn on the ignition in a closed garage? Didn't Sylvia Plath turn on the oven? Didn't Bessie Smith die with a quarter in her hand after earning millions? Decades passed before we discovered that she was refused admission by a whites-only hospital in the midst of a heart attack. At the outset, the fact that Marilyn Monroe was naked was the most salient point of her death. This detail. That dying—that at her last moment in her most desperate privacy she had surrendered herself not only to the Los Angeles police but to the world. There were no photographs published but for the million minds who photographed her nudity upon a bed, none were necessary. The whole world saw her at last—stark naked.

Now they had seen everything—would they pity? Only gradually and only after they had sated themselves, masticating on till there was nothing left but the divine husk. Then they could worship it. The woman gone, the human being done in and destroyed, they took a step back and appropriated her as a goddess. Forever young and Anglo-Saxon, eternally even if artificially blond, forever smiling with a pretended happiness about her luscious mouth. It is the mouth Warhol goes for, multiplies over and over, playing upon the implications of fellatio in this opened and ecstatic orifice.

The very fact of her suffering is excluded by the glorious image. The anguish of her end, the loss of face, the despair of her perceived failure, the artist's own judg-

82  ment against herself, surrendering, concurring finally with the guys. The hot shots and authorities, all the big and little Strasbergs, the sneering and envious, even actors who would never be as beautiful and knew it. The crowded world itself who took the image she had created—imposed upon her, yes, but then improved upon the comedienne until it transcended itself—for reality. And then denied that it was art.

The happy girl gave up. Only then could she be forgiven. Woman made flesh, punished and used and derided.

## THE "LOVE GODDESS" WHO NEVER FOUND ANY LOVE

*Clare Boothe Luce*

*E*arly on Sunday morning, August 5, 1962, Marilyn Monroe died by her own hand. The suicide of this radiant woman, "The Love Goddess of the Nuclear Age," was splashed across the front pages of the world and produced an orgy of public commentary. Editorialists, political commentators, creative writers, dramatic and literary critics, fellow artists, friends, and foes seemed obsessed by the question of why this woman, possessing beauty, fame, and money in such abundance, had so feared or hated life that she could no longer face it.

She was identified as an innocent victim. It was widely felt that somehow she had been condemned and driven to her death as surely as any hapless aristocrat condemned by the tribunal of the French Revolution was driven in the tumbrels to the guillotine. And in the days following her death, the sob sisters and gossip writers gave a fine imitation of the Old Ladies of the Guillotine who gleefully knitted while counting every head that fell into the basket. But although views differed as to who or what had condemned and finally executed her, Hollywood was far and away the most favored villain.

In Moscow, *Izvestia* commented that Hollywood "gave birth to her, and it killed her." New York's *Daily Worker* indicted the capitalistic motion picture producers who "turn woman into a piece of meat," and sell not only the bodies but also the "souls of their fellow human beings." The Vatican's *L'Osservatore Romano* put the blame on the general decline of morals, holding that Marilyn was the victim of a godless way of life of which Hollywood "forced her to be the symbol." Britain's *Manchester Guardian* saw her as the victim of her fans, forever haunted by "a nightmare of herself 60 feet tall and naked before the howling mob." The *New York Times* blamed the Hollywood star system. "The sad and ironic realization," said the *Times,* "is that Miss Monroe aspired to creativity. . . . But the effort to overcome the many obstacles . . . was apparently too great for her. Therein lies her tragedy and Hollywood's."

On the second anniversary of Marilyn Monroe's death, perhaps what most wants saying is that whoever or whatever killed Marilyn, it was *not* Hollywood. The easy acceptance of Hollywood as the author of her tragedy has obscured whatever meaning and moral her life and death may have for the public.

Hollywood brought Marilyn Monroe fame, money, adulation, two respected and also famous husbands (Joe DiMaggio and Arthur Miller), and the help, however belatedly sought, of competent psychiatrists. But for all these, Marilyn might have gone to her death in her twenties instead of her thirties.

Indeed, the "howling mob" who made her see herself as "60 feet tall and naked" gave her the only form of sustained emotional security she ever knew, or perhaps was capable of understanding. For if her public saw her as a "Love Goddess" to whom limitless love was owed, that is the way she saw herself in her happiest hours—most of them Hollywood hours.

A FEW WEEKS before she died, Marilyn told *Life:* "I think that sexuality is only attractive when it's natural. . . . We are all born sexual creatures, thank God, but it's a pity so many people despise and crush this natural gift. Art, real art, comes from it—everything. I never understood it—this sex symbol—I always thought symbols were those things you clash together! That's the trouble, a sex symbol becomes a thing—I just hate to be a thing. If I'm going to be a symbol of something, I'd rather have it sex. . . ."

At the conscious level, Marilyn believed that her extraordinary power to project sex was her great gift. Her despair at the end was perhaps akin to that of a painter who discovers he is going blind, or of a pianist whose hands are becoming arthritic. The threatened loss of a great talent or functional capacity that a person sees as the paramount meaning of his life—the "reason why" of his being—has often led to a suicide.

Whatever else Marilyn had hoped—and failed—to find in life, her "howling" public must have been what she feared to lose when she reached out for her last and lethal dose of barbiturates. Surely she realized that the mob worship of her for her pure sexuality could not last more than a few years longer. Breasts, belly, bottom must one day sag. She was thirty-six, and her mirror had begun to warn her.

A girl entering her teens, especially an American girl, has intense, secret, often lengthy encounters with a looking glass. They are a legitimate manifestation of every unmarried girl's concern for her future as wife and mother. She learns early that the male has a natural preference for young and pretty women. But too often she continues, even after marriage and motherhood, to believe that *who* she is is *what* she looks like in her mirror. Advertising spends billions of dollars fostering this essentially immature attitude in adult women. For, the more mature and emotionally secure a woman becomes, the less she turns to the looking glass to give her self-confidence and a sense of her own personhood, and the more she looks into the eyes of the people she loves and who love her for the true reflection of her identity.

But the narcissistic approach to a mirror is a continuing, ever-more-urgent professional necessity for a movie star who is celebrated, rewarded, and adored for her physical attractions. Her daily, often hourly encounters with her "mirror, mirror on the wall," however satisfying and reassuring in the beginning, become summit meetings with her archenemy—time.

After Marilyn passed thirty, her sessions with her studio mirror must have been increasingly agonizing experiences. The growing hostility and aggressiveness she began to show in her later years, especially to men who worked with her, and the endless changes of clothes and protracted primpings in her dressing room, the fits of vomiting just before the cameras began to grind—all these may have foreshadowed her terror of that hour when her multiple lover, the wolf-whistling mobs of men and oohing-and-aahing women would desert her.

What, then, would make her valuable, even in her own eyes? Who was Marilyn Monroe if not that lovely girl on the screen, that delectable creature she saw in the mirror?

"Everything is so wonderful—people are so kind," she once said in one of her triumphant hours. "But I feel as though it's all happening to someone right next to

*all the available light*

me. I'm close—I can feel it, I can hear it, but it isn't really *me*."

Marilyn knew who the "real me" was. But this was an admission she sought to escape. Her efforts to become a dramatic actress, to interest herself in literature and music, the pathetic efforts she made to adopt the religion of her third husband, Arthur Miller, and to transform herself into his intellectual companion and a good little housewife were certainly a part of her valiant effort to escape this "real me"—who was one of the saddest and most frightened little girls ever born—Norma Jeane Mortensen.[1]

MARILYN'S FATE, LIKE her body, began to take shape while she still lay in her mother's womb. But unlike her body, the shape it took from the beginning was not lovely. An ugly congeries of evil fairies—insanity, illegitimacy, infidelity, promiscuity, ignorance, and poverty—presided over her cradle.

Her mother, Mrs. Gladys Baker, was a pretty red-haired twenty-four-year-old woman who worked as a film cutter for RKO. Mrs. Baker's father and mother had been in mental institutions and a brother had committed suicide. She had married Baker when she was fifteen, and borne him two children. He deserted her a few years later, taking his children with him. A succession of men followed him in Mrs. Baker's bed, including one Edward Mortensen, an itinerant bread-baker. The child of this casual union was born on June 1, 1926, in Los Angeles, and baptized Norma Jeane Mortensen. The father was not present: he disappeared, and forever, the day Gladys Baker told him she was pregnant.

Throughout her life, Marilyn Monroe was haunted by the enigma of her paternity. Of all the stories Marilyn ever told about herself, perhaps the most touching concerned what happened when she met President Kennedy at his 1962 birthday rally in Madison Square Garden, where she had been invited to sing "Happy Birthday." Afterward, she proudly attended the reception with Arthur Miller's seventy-seven-year-old father, Isadore Miller. "I think I did something wrong when I met the President," she said. "Instead of saying, 'How do you do,' I just said, 'This is my former father-in-law, Isadore Miller.'" Marilyn then explained that she had presented her former husband's father to the president because he was an "immigrant" and "I thought this would be one of the biggest things in his life. . . ." The chances are, it was the biggest thing in Marilyn's life to say the word "father" to the president, even though her father was an ex–in-law.

Following the birth of her child, Gladys Baker returned to her job. In her moody and feckless fashion, she cared for Norma Jeane during the first few years of her infancy. Then she began to give evidence of violent mental disturbance and was committed to an institution. Norma Jeane was made a ward of the County of Los Angeles. For the next four or five years, she was farmed out by the County Welfare Agency to a series of foster parents, who were paid $20 a month. None of her foster homes apparently offered her even the barest security, much less love. The pattern of anxiety, hostility, and moral confusion that underlay all Marilyn's human relations in later life was indelibly set in these early childhood years.

"I always felt insecure and in the way," she once said, "but most of all I felt scared. . . . I guess I wanted love more than anything in the world."

AT THE AGE of seven or eight, in one of these "homes," Norma Jeane was seduced by an elderly star boarder. She recalled in later years that he was an old man who wore a heavy golden watch chain over the wide expanse of his vest, and that he gave her a nickel "not to tell." When she nevertheless did tell, the woman who was her foster mother at the time severely punished her for making up lies about the "fine man." The unhealthy and confused emotional correlations she made all through her life among sex, money, and guilt may have stemmed in part from this ugly first encounter with man's lust. After the punishment she suffered for the rape of her innocence, she acquired a stammer that remained with her throughout her life.

Mother Gladys Baker was released from the asylum when Norma Jeane was eight, got a job, and took her daughter back to live with her. But a year later, she became violent again and was recommitted. Since then, except for brief periods, Mrs. Baker's pitiful life has been spent in mental institutions.

At the age of nine, Norma Jeane was sent to an orphanage. There she earned nickels by washing dishes and cleaning toilets. The fairy-tale Cinderella, sweeping ashes from the hearth, lived a normal, protected, happy life compared with that of this rootless little orphan of the City of the Angels. When Norma Jeane was eleven, an old friend of her mother, Grace McKee Goddard, rescued her from the orphanage. Mrs. Goddard sent her to live with her aunt, Miss Ana Lower, in Sawtelle, a Los Angeles slum, and later took her in herself. This was about the only period in all her youth when she knew even a semblance of security and affection.

In those years, Norma Jeane, like millions of other small girls, also dreamed of becoming a movie star. But Norma Jeane had a special gift. It began to manifest itself when she was twelve. One morning, before going to school, she decided to put on lipstick, eyebrow pencil, and a borrowed blue sweater one size too small for her. "My arrival in school started everybody buzzing," she recalled. "The boys began screaming and groaning. . . . Even the girls paid a little attention to me." Norma Jeane discovered, to her great delight, the one dazzling gift that had been bestowed on her at birth—an exuberant, vital, almost atomic capacity to project her sexuality. Marilyn Monroe was in the making.

She married for the first time in 1942, when she was

barely sixteen. Her husband, James Dougherty, then twenty-one, seems to have been an ordinary "decent Joe." (He is now on the Los Angeles police force.) In later years, he recalled that she was a good cook, but she did not give him the feeling of self-esteem and self-confidence a man needs to keep even a sexual liaison going, much less a marriage. James Dougherty and Norma Jeane separated in 1944, apparently without tears. When he shipped overseas in the Merchant Marine, she divorced him in Las Vegas and went to work as a paint sprayer in a Los Angeles defense plant.

WHAT MARILYN'S SEX life was like in the days before she sought to storm the golden gates of Hollywood can only be surmised. It cannot, even by today's easy standards, have been "moral." For she had no father or mother image to guide her as to the proper behavior of boys and girls. Never having known the face of marital or parental or even fraternal love, she was certainly incapable of giving what she herself had never known.

In a posthumously published interview, which took place during the first year of her marriage to Arthur Miller, Marilyn offered this explanation: "I guess I was soured on marriage because all I knew was men who swore at their wives, and fathers who never played with their kids. The husbands I remember from my childhood got drunk regularly, and the wives were always drab women who never had a chance to dress or make up or be taken anywhere to have fun. I grew up thinking, 'If this is marriage, who needs it?'"

In the same interview, Marilyn said, "Gee, I love being married [to Arthur Miller]! All my life I've been alone. Now for the first time, the really first time, I feel I'm not alone any more. For the first time I have a feeling of being sheltered. It's as if I have come in out of the cold. . . . There's a feeling of being together—a warmth and tenderness. I don't mean a display of affection or anything like that. I mean just being together."

THIS, OF COURSE, was not a mature woman speaking of deep intellectual and physical union in marriage. It was the orphan child speaking—the child who was still seeking a permanent home where warmth and tenderness would always be given unconditionally by the "grown-ups," in this case by Arthur Miller.

The young Norma Jeane was also always trying to avoid the cold. Despising marriage, deeply distrustful of both men and women but nevertheless hungry to the core of her being for admiration, affection, and acceptance as a person, she sought "love" with what must have been a fever-pitch promiscuity. Indeed, by the time she was entering womanhood, a miracle was needed to save her from a life of overt and covert prostitution. That miracle happened. Its name was Hollywood.

In 1945, she found employment with the Blue Books Model Agency in Los Angeles as a photographers' model. The agency advised her to dye her dark blond hair a golden blond. Within a year, her face, ringed with golden curls—and great peachy reaches of her body—had become familiar and welcome items in all the men's magazines from *Laff* to *Pic*. Soon a screen test was arranged for her and she was signed by Twentieth Century-Fox. Cameraman Leon Shamroy reminisced some years later that "every frame of the test radiated sex." These pristine radiations of a Love Goddess did not, however, reach the public. After playing a bit part in *Scudda Hoo! Scudda Hay!*—which some latter-day Gladys Baker left on the cutting-room floor—she was dropped by Fox. The only professional step forward she seems to have made in her twentieth year was a second change of name. Norma Jeane Mortensen Baker Dougherty became Marilyn Monroe.

When she was twenty-two, she got an assignment from Columbia, the lead in an obscure B picture called *Ladies of the Chorus,* which was shot in eleven days. And it was during this time that the movie magazines first recorded a Marilyn Monroe "romance," with Fred Karger, a musical director (and now husband of Jane Wyman). But the end to this romance revealed, for the first time, that she was already flirting with another escort—death. After the romance failed, she made her first of several attempts at suicide. The rejection of her physical person could not have failed to trigger and wildly intensify the deep-rooted feelings of nonbelongingness, unworthiness, and unwantedness ingrained in her by her miserable childhood.

Marilyn's first big movie break came when Arthur Hornblow, Jr., and John Huston were trying to cast the minor role of Louis Calhern's mistress in *The Asphalt Jungle*. It called for an angel-faced blonde with a wickedly curvaceous figure. Marilyn was tested for the part, and on neither score was she found wanting. Hornblow recalls that she arrived on the set "scared half to death" and dressed as "a cheap tart."

"As soon as we saw her, we knew she was the one," he said, but "we had to strip that all the way down to get to the basic girl, the real quality, the true Lolita quality." This time Hollywood was not looking for mere "meat"; it was looking for the quality that would at once touch the heart, evoking tenderness, and race the blood, stirring all the senses. This was the quality of innocent depravity and it can be found only in a female "juvenile delinquent." Marilyn had that quality. Hollywood simply recognized it.

Her part in *The Asphalt Jungle* got her movie career onto the ways. But again, to exculpate Hollywood of forcing her to become a sex symbol, it should be remembered the picture that first made her famous had nothing to do with the movies. It was a photograph of Marilyn in the nude, for which she had cheerfully posed when she was modeling, a year before she appeared in *The Asphalt Jungle.* Asked, years after the shot had been circulated worldwide, what she had on when she posed for it, she replied, "The radio."

The photographer paid Marilyn $50 for posing, sold the picture for $500 to John Baumgarth, publisher of calendars, who reputedly made $750,000 out of it. (The nickel rate established by the star boarder was maintained throughout her life. Her sex appeal, which grossed over $100 million for Hollywood, left her with about $500,000 when she died.) This unidentified photograph, which Mr. Baumgarth prophetically called *Golden Dreams,* was a best-seller. The public became aware of the fact that Marilyn was the calendar girl just as her film *Clash by Night* was about to be released. The Fox brass blew their tops and threatened to drop her. Facing again the old foster parent/star boarder pattern of rejection and punishment for a misdemeanor involving sex, Marilyn once more talked of suicide. But this time the "howling mob" and the conquering wolf whistle came to her rescue. After seeing *Golden Dreams,* the public clamored to see still more of Marilyn's charms— even though there weren't, really, any more to be seen. Thus, she and the public, not Hollywood, launched her career as the Love Goddess.

Years later she said, "When I was a little girl, maybe 6 or 7, I dreamed of standing up in church without any clothes on, naked and with no sense of sin." Her rationalization of this dream was that she probably "wanted to take my clothes off because I was ashamed of them. They were orphan's clothes. Naked, I was like any other girl." The point was—and *Golden Dreams* made it—that naked, Marilyn was *not* like any other girl. In terms of nakedness alone, she was sheer female perfection, and she knew it and rejoiced in it. "Men," she once said happily, "feel as if they want to spend *all* night with me!" That the desire to spend *all* night with her was something different from the desire to spend all of a lifetime with her she never, perhaps, quite understood—even after the collapse of her three marriages.

The story of Marilyn's years of stardom as the Love Goddess are too well known to need repeating. But behind the façade of the gay and happy star, this "basic girl," the tragic Lolita, remained unchanged and unchangeable.

A YEAR AND a half after Marilyn's suicide, the question of "Who killed Marilyn?" was unexpectedly revived by a competent witness—her third husband, playwright Arthur Miller. In his autobiographical and self-defensive play *After the Fall,* produced last January, Miller, not surprisingly, finds that whoever else was "responsible" for Marilyn's death, it certainly was *not* Arthur Miller. But neither does Miller blame Hollywood. He holds that Marilyn wrought her own destruction by insisting on seeing herself as the utterly helpless victim of her parents, her loves and husbands, her profession and her friends—a victim who, in her own eyes, could be "saved" only by a "limitless love." Miller's gloss on this—and one of the themes of his play—is that while every man is his brother's (and sister's) keeper, no man could give "limitless love" even to the loveliest and neediest of women. Especially not Arthur Miller who, as the play demonstrates, has quite a few unresolved problems of his own in the love-unlimited department.

There is no reason to dispute Miller's self-exculpation of the tragedy of the woman he brought to bed as his wife for four troubled years and to whom he sincerely tried to give enough of his mind and heart to make any normal woman feel "sheltered." If, at first, he saw himself somewhat egotistically in relationship to her as a combination of Romeo, Pygmalion, and Dr. Freud, this mistake was probably born of the same basically idealistic impulses that led him in his early days to flirt with communism. To his credit, he recognized fairly early the fatuousness of his attempt to play "Savior" to Marilyn's ambivalent "Magdalene." He encouraged her to seek psychiatric help to bolster her self-esteem by developing whatever gifts she believed she might have as an actress.

Hollywood's reactions to Marilyn's latter-day dramatic aspirations were cruel. One producer voices this judgment on her dramatic chances: "Act? That blonde can't act her way out of a Whirlpool bra!" Mike Todd called her "the greatest con artist of them all." And Billy Wilder, who was her director in *The Seven Year Itch* and

*Some Like It Hot,* and one of the few in Hollywood she respected, was quoted: "The question is whether Marilyn is a person at all, or one of the greatest Du Pont products ever invented. She has breasts like granite, and a brain like Swiss cheese, full of holes. . . . The charm of her is her two left feet." Asked if he wanted to direct a third film with her, he said, "I am too old and too rich to go through this again."

PERHAPS THESE JUDGMENTS on Marilyn's dramatic talents were as false as they were harsh. But it was certainly true that Marilyn did not have the self-control or self-discipline to become a Broadway dramatic star.

Arthur Miller has accurately identified some of the causes that led to her three divorces, her many troubles with her studio, and eventually to her suicide: the insatiable demands for "limitless love," the moodiness and depressions, the orgies of self-recrimination alternated with orgies of recrimination of others, the clearly self-destructive urges, which were always boiling and seething under the bubbling, slapdash mask of careless, vibrant, even rapturous happiness she tried to project to the public.

Marilyn died, really, on a Saturday night. The girl whose translucent beauty had made her the "love object" of millions of unknown lonely or unsatisfied males had no date that evening.

Apparently, none of the men or women she knew well had, in the end, cared enough for her to "hang around" and try to cheer her up, although everyone knew she was suffering, physically and mentally. And Marilyn evidently neither loved nor trusted anyone enough to seek help.

Above all, Marilyn was profoundly suspicious of the motives of everyone in her own regard. It was why she walked like a cat, alone, in the midnight alleys of her soul, rejecting lovers and friends before they could get around—as her mother and all her foster parents had done—to rejecting her. She had an almost psychopathic fear of being "used," financially used, as she had first been used by the foster parents who tolerated her only because she brought $20 board money; sexually used, as she was used by the man who gave her a nickel for the first display of her sex; professionally used, as in the nature of their business, by producers and agents. No doubt she convinced herself that she had been "used" by her two famous husbands. The egos of Joe DiMaggio and Arthur Miller may have been flattered by their public procession of America's Love Goddess, but they certainly were not flattened. There is little question but that both men gave her more love, tenderness, and understanding than they received. When she died, she set up a $100,000 trust fund for her mother. But she left the bulk of her estate to her dramatic coach, Lee Strasberg, and to Marianne Kris, one of her psychiatrists. She must have seen them as the only people who had earnestly sought to help her escape from Norma Jeane Mortensen and find a new identity when her Love Goddess days would be over.

It is interesting to reflect what Marilyn Monroe might think of *After the Fall*. It would, perhaps, trigger every ambivalent reaction and emotion ingrained in her by her childhood. Morbidly sensitive to exploitation, she would probably be cruelly hurt that her own husband (once a passionately dedicated critic of Hollywood's "values") had gone into the business of selling her, body and soul, to the public—and as badly damaged sexy goods. But certainly she would be pleased to find that her "image" still packed a punch with the public. Pathetically eager at the end to be taken "seriously" on Broadway, she would be proud to find her "image" seriously presented in a dramatic work of some intellectual distinction. Perhaps the fact that her former husband had achieved his success—after a long period of artistic impotence—by "using" her would, even while hurting her, please her. It might give her that ambivalent sense of superiority that people often experience when they can feel that someone they have looked up to or trusted has let them down.

IN THE PLAY, Miller makes her say, "I'm a joke that brings in money." Marilyn would consider it the cream of the jest that, even after her death, the joke is still a big moneymaker. For when Hollywood is done with *After the Fall,* Marilyn's ghostly ears will once again hear the music she loved best—the loud, lusty masculine wolf whistles of her adoring public.

It was not the scope of Miller's play, and it is not the scope of this article, to define where Marilyn Monroe's tragedy, in the words of Moscow's *Izvestia,* "transcended personal limits and had social reverberations." But of course, there were instant—and tragic—reverberations to it. The suicide rate in Los Angeles County jumped 40 percent during the three weeks of "hot" publicity given her death. Those suicides who identified with her may have felt "doomed," as she felt herself to be, to a suicidal solution of their problems. Others, depressed over their lack of money, fame, youth, or sex, may have asked themselves, "If she, the woman who had 'everything' had nothing to live for, what do I, with so much less, have to live for?"

For all its "corn," the simplest lesson of Marilyn's life is that children need parents, or parent substitutes, who not only love them but who love and respect one another. Without this greatest of all cradle gifts, a happy home, it is all but impossible for them in adulthood to deal with either of those two impostors—failure and success.

Cinderella lives happily ever after only in the fairy tale. In real life, no matter how many clothes she puts on—or takes off—her heart remains embittered and her spirit soiled by the ashes she swept in childhood.

# LOOKING GOOD

*Marge Piercy*

*I* approach her with boredom and disquiet, as if circling an exotic dump of fifties paraphernalia, Freudian texts, merry widows, brassieres built like rocket launchers, spike heels four inches high, canisters of hair spray the consistency of shellac, back-alley abortions you tell no one about, marriage as the Holy Grail, ruffled aprons, and plucked eyebrows. So much verbiage swirls around her, so many egos have flirted with and co-opted her ghost, at first there seems little at the center but a vacuum.

Marilyn Monroe can be approached as Norma Jeane, as the woman her neighbor in bungalow 31, Simone Signoret, said took three hours to turn herself into "Marilyn." Her work can be critiqued cinematically, with an appreciation of her underrated work as a comic actress—always denigrated not for her beauty which was granted but for her talent. She can be treated as an icon, what she presented on the screen and in her life as people imagined it and what was dreamed into that icon by all those whose eyes and lust tried to possess her.

It was necessary to overlook her talent, her intelligence, her ambition, because part of what men read into her and what indeed she presented was a child in a woman's body—the breathy voice that so famously embodies that vulnerability, the inability to protect herself. She was presented as much thing as woman in the gaze of the camera, whether film or still. There is a certain sadism aroused by her in all her incarnations, from Norma Jeane to "Marilyn." She recognized that victim radiance in herself. You cannot imagine her by any stretch of the imagination playing Joan Crawford's role in *Johnny Guitar* or any of Katharine Hepburn's roles where her body speaks intelligence and will. Marilyn cannot attack. She cannot even defend. She can suffer, she can be protected, she can wish and yearn. But hidden in all that white breathiness is the woman who survived rape, abuse, being handed from powerful man to powerful man like a bottle of gin, and who wanted and studied hard to be a good actress.

She seems at once to flaunt herself and to cringe within her shell. She creates in us a power as she seems powerless, the sense that she exists to be looked at, to be consumed by the public and the private gaze. If she is not looked at, not desired, not consumed by our gaze, she may disappear; and she did. We do not imagine her making speeches or walking a picket line or supporting candidates, although she had politics; we may define her by her absence or desire to be absent: her famous tardiness, her desire to escape the gaze that defined her, the many suicide attempts and the ambiguity about the final successful act—whether it was one more gesture that got out of hand, or a completed act.

One thing that may strike a woman upon viewing her old movies is that she was one of the last female stars who had a woman's natural body. She would be told now immediately to go on a strict diet and sent for liposuction, because we are no longer supposed to look womanly. Today's stars are carved and bony. She jiggled. She swayed. She was ripe and succulent. If she had bones, they were buried in flesh. She was flesh itself made luminous. Muscles, bones, sinews, they were there but unimportant in the message of flesh and skin, the softest moon glowing out of her ridiculous dresses. A woman could look at her and admire the sugar-cake "Marilyn"—the artifact of bleach and the expert teasing of a hairdresser, the makeup, the foundation like an iron maiden, the dresses she was sewn into—and still feel that on a good day and with kind lighting "I could look something like that." Because a woman could be sure that she could exude some of that appeal in her natural body. Few women can feel that confidence about size-zero icons of today. It was opulence, not discipline and starvation, that Marilyn Monroe embodied, but a tainted opulence for other women.

The women she played were totally unreal. Her vulnerability in her flesh was as compelling and audible as a baby crying, but she played either a gold digger—the woman who can *only* be bought—or the child/whore who asks nothing whatsoever, who is available as a tray of hors d'oeuvres at the cocktail party. In *The Seven Year Itch,* she is the total male fantasy of available snatch, a gorgeous woman without any entanglements, no friends, no family, no demands, wants only a married man since he won't fall in love with her. What living woman could ever identify with that character?

She was valued for her face and its beauty, certainly, but far more she was desired for her body. A woman whose body is desired while she herself—her real past, her ambitions, her fears, her ideas—is ignored, develops a deeply ambivalent relationship with that body. It does not quite belong to her, but rather to those who value it beyond her, and all she seems to have to offer them is that same body. It is always a fraught relationship, because the body bloats, grows or shrinks, has its own mind, produces a period—in her case, incredibly painful—or doesn't (her confessed many abortions), gets pregnant or refuses to; demands food, demands sleep and then refuses to enter it; worst of all, threatens to grow older, and will, and will. Furthermore, she remembers when she was far from cherished, when she was scorned, mocked, abused, unwanted. That is who, she suspects, she really is, under this dress of skin others want to touch. This body is what they all want, but she suspects herself of being a fraud, because inside is just her. Maybe that self-hatred and that wearing of the body as total presentation was the reason she reportedly could not reach orgasm.[1] She had to please; she did not deserve pleasure. She could not ask for pleasure for herself, only attention: what a child can demand. For if you are only your body, you are meat; you are cunt; you are what men most desire and most despise. That despisement she felt all the way through to her spine. The gaze that brought her into existence as "Marilyn" and kept her in existence just as long as she could keep that gaze on her, was also a judgmental and pricing gaze. If I were a graphic artist, I would draw a Marilyn butterfly pinned by an eye-headed stake. But the voice also matters in this creation.

I remember a friend and I hearing ourselves on radio in the late sixties, when we were putting on the Students for a Democratic Society radio show in New York, and discovering how like little girls we sounded. We worked very hard to get rid of those high voices and those helpless, mirthless girlish giggles—because we wanted to be taken seriously. So did she, but to abandon the façade of cotton candy would be to lose all that had made her famous and desirable. What it takes to lower the voice is not to "put on" another voice, but to relax the diaphragm and throat—to let go, in a way, to assume a kind of authority with one's body.

Her career began with the infamous nude calendar, although her most lasting images are at once dressed and undressed—the pose on the subway grating, for instance. She wears a flimsy halter dress that flies up, deserting her. She is the embodiment of titillation. Any man can dream of possessing her, because she seems so accessible and defenseless. For a man, that image on which can be projected any fantasy, any wish fulfillment, is the source of her immense and lasting appeal. She is a living doll— the perfect body that offers everything and asks nothing. She embodies the woman who never was because she isn't anything in herself. That image was something she put on to go out into the frightening and hostile world. She had learned early that she would be rewarded if she appeared compliant and childlike, not in the sense of the virgin to be deflowered, but in the sense of the woman who doesn't understand, doesn't know what to do, never learns a lesson, warm and sensual Galatea to any chance Pygmalion, a living warm statue who never gets up and leaves but waits passively for the next owner. But behind that façade was a woman needy, scared, ambitious, leaking self-hatred and desperately wanting something real and solid and important. She wanted to be . . . respected. She never was.

# golden girl:
# marilyn in hollywood

She was for a time Hollywood's darling, the goose that laid not just a single golden egg, but a whole bevy of them. Though they have been called slight, Marilyn Monroe's films are nevertheless given weight and validity by the sheer heft of her inimitable presence in them. Even her seemingly minor roles—a crooked politician's mistress in *The Asphalt Jungle,* a would-be starlet with a jittery stomach in *All About Eve*—have elicited reams of commentary; Monroe's major film roles have generated even more.

When Molly Haskell's groundbreaking book *From Reverence to Rape: The Treatment of Women in the Movies* first appeared in 1974, it was considered a radical departure from the kinds of academic, feminist film theory and criticism that had preceded it. Instead, Haskell had an easygoing, accessible style that both welcomed and wowed the reader. In the excerpt that appears here, Haskell deploys her considerable knowledge and understanding of American film to comment on Monroe's movie roles, and the ways in which they both reflected and shaped the media's tumultuous relationship to women.

But an academic analysis of Monroe's film work still has much to offer, as is evidenced by scholar and professor Sabrina Barton's "Face Value." Rather than treat the subject of Monroe's film career in its entirety, Barton's discussion is primarily restricted to Monroe's performance (a word which Barton claims has multiple levels of meaning) in two famous comedies. According to Barton, the characters played by Monroe in both *Gentlemen Prefer Blondes* and *How to Marry a Millionaire* subvert the expected notions of femininity (passivity, dependence on male approval, lack of intellect) and instead present us with unlikely paradigms of female strength, empowerment, and autonomy.

Viennese-born novelist and essayist Lore Segal treats Monroe's film roles in an entirely different framework. "Sexy and Her Sisters" posits two enduring female types: the pretty girl and the plain (or ugly) one, who have traditionally paired together—think of Cinderella and her stepsisters. According to Segal, each of these types has her own virtues and/or attributes. But again, Monroe upsets and subverts expectations by assuming the best qualities of each.

The final selection in this section is a chapter excerpted from Sir Laurence Olivier's autobiography, *Confessions of an Actor,* which reconstructs the making of *The Prince and the Showgirl.* At the time, the idea of casting the bombshell with the thespian was cause for enormous Hollywood buzz. Clearly, Olivier and Monroe each felt they had something to gain by association with the other. In Monroe's case, it was the artistic legitimacy conferred by Olivier's incomparable theatrical gifts. In Olivier's, it may have been the glitter of Monroe's stardust, which he hoped would rub off on his own shoulders. In addition to his illustrious career playing Shakespeare's heroes and villains, Olivier also made his share of what self-styled student of the Monroe phenomenon Ernest Cunningham calls "movie rubbish." In Cunningham's view, Olivier was probably slumming when he agreed to do *The Prince and the Showgirl;* Olivier was known to have said, "Nothing is beneath me if it pays well. I've earned the right to damn well grab whatever I can in the time I've got left." In the excerpt that appears here, Olivier paints himself in an understandably flattering light, though others, including Cunningham and Arthur Miller, describe the palpable

*all the available light*

tension on the set as *The Prince and the Showgirl* was be-ing filmed. Still, many people (including Dennis Grunes, whose essay appears later in this volume), now feel that Monroe triumphed by giving a lovely performance, while Olivier's has gone down in film history as priggish and stodgy.

## WE WOULD HAVE HAD TO
## INVENT HER
*Molly Haskell*

*O*ur feelings about Marilyn Monroe have been so colored by her death and not simply, as the uncharitable would have us think, because she is no longer an irritation or a threat, but because her suicide, as suicides do, casts a retrospective light on her life. Her "ending" gives her a beginning and middle, turns her into a work of art with a message and a meaning.

Women, particularly, have become contrite over their previous hostility to Monroe, canonizing her as a martyr to male chauvinism, which in most ways she was. But at the time, women couldn't identify with her and didn't support her. They allowed her to be turned into a figure of ridicule, as they allowed Ingrid Bergman to be crucified by the press. They blamed these stars for acting disadvantageously, whereas they sympathized with Rita Hayworth and Elizabeth Taylor for moving (in the words applied to *That Hamilton Woman*) "lower and lower but always up and up." At the same time, in their defense, women hated Marilyn for catering so shamelessly to a false, regressive, childish, and detached idea of sexuality.

What was she, this breathless, blond, supplicating symbol of sexuality, the lips anxiously offering themselves as the surrogate orifice, the whisper unconsciously expressing trepidation? And who made her what she was? She was partly a hypothesis, a pinup fantasy of the other woman as she might be drawn in the marital cartoon fantasies of Maggie and Jiggs, or Blondie and Dagwood, and thus an outgrowth, once again, of misogyny. She was the woman that every wife fears seeing with her husband in a convertible (Hawks's *Monkey Business*) or even in conversation, and that every emasculated or superfluous husband would like to think his wife lives in constant fear of. She was the masturbatory fantasy that gave satisfaction and demanded nothing in return; the wolf bait, the eye-stopper that men exchanged glances over; the erotic sex-and-glamour symbol to Easterners like Arthur Miller turned on by the Hollywood vulgarity the way Nabokov was by that temple of philistinism, the American motel.

The times being what they were, if she hadn't existed, we would have had to invent her, and we did, in a way. She was the fifties' fiction, the lie that a woman has no sexual needs, that she is there to cater to, or enhance, a man's needs. She was the living embodiment of half of one of the more grotesque and familiar pseudocouples—the old man and the "showgirl," immortalized in *Esquire* and *Playboy* cartoons.

The difference between Monroe and the archetypal brassy blonde is the difference between Monroe and Jayne Mansfield, the real cartoon of overblown sex appeal, the fifties' synecdoche (with the part, or rather pair, standing for the whole) whose comic grotesqueness was exploited, with complementary male absurdities, by Frank Tashlin in *Will Success Spoil Rock Hunter?* and *The Girl Can't Help It*. Unlike Mansfield, Monroe's heart wasn't in it; they—the cartoon blondes—are hard, but she was soft.

She catered to these fantasies and played these roles because she was afraid that if she stopped—which she did once and for all with sleeping pills—there would turn out to be nothing there, and therefore nothing to love. She was never permitted to mature into a warm, vibrant woman, or fully use her gifts for comedy, despite the signals and flares she kept sending up. Instead, she was turned into a figure of mockery in the parts she played and to the men she played with. In *The Asphalt Jungle* and *All About Eve*, she was a sex object and nincompoop. In *How to Marry a Millionaire, We're Not Mar-*

*all the available light*

*ried, The Seven Year Itch,* and *Niagara,* she was paired with sexless leading men (David Wayne, David Wayne, Tom Ewell, Joseph Cotten) while the other women (Bacall and Grable in *How to Marry,* for example) were given reasonable partners. In *Bus Stop,* with its covertly homosexual patterns, she played a parody earth mother to Don Murray's innocent stud. In Hawks's *Monkey Business* and *Gentlemen Prefer Blondes,* she played a tootsie who is most comfortable with older men (Charles Coburn in both) and little boys (Cary Grant as a regressed scientist and George Winslow as a real youngster). In *Some Like It Hot,* her leading man—Tony Curtis—did a Cary Grant imitation, and was thus a "bogus" romantic lead. In her "serious" roles, in *Don't Bother to Knock* and *Niagara,* she was a psychopath, while Anne Bancroft and Jean Peters played the normal women. When she finally played an ex–saloon singer with brains and feelings who *evolves* emotionally (Preminger's *River of No Return,* opposite Robert Mitchum), the film was a flop: audiences wouldn't accept her as a real woman. In *Let's Make Love,* she played a silly Cinderella to Yves Montand's millionaire. And in *The Prince and the Showgirl* and *The Misfits,* playing opposite Olivier and Gable, her image as sexpot and/or psychopath, as it had already evolved from her Fox films, was treated almost in the abstract, that is, was accepted, unquestioned, as her identity.

And yet, throughout her career, she was giving more to idiotic parts than they called for—more feeling, more warmth, more anguish; and, as a result, her films have a richer tone than they deserve. The best ones, which is to say the best she could get under the circumstances, are the films that suggest the discrepancy between the woman (and young girl) and the sexpot, even as their directors (Wilder and Hawks) exploit the image, through exaggeration, more than they have to—though still more gently than other directors.

In Billy Wilder's *Some Like It Hot,* Tony Curtis and Jack Lemmon are musicians who, dressed as women, flee Chicago with an all-girl orchestra to escape the mob, as they have inadvertently witnessed a gangland rubout. Their "transvestism" or sexual inversion matches Marilyn's excesses, on the one hand, and Joe E. Brown's "recesses" on the other.[1] Too blond and buxom, Marilyn is as much "in drag" as they are, a child playing the monumentally daffy, all-American blond tootsie. She finds in Lemmon her soulmate—a little girl like herself playing grown-up; but in Curtis she finds the sexual casualty (the would-be leading man to match her would-be leading lady) whose strengths match her weaknesses and weaknesses her strengths. They become "lovers" after their own fashion, while, in a parody of Marilyn's usual film fate, Lemmon plays sugar daughter to Joe E. Brown's sugar daddy, and one relationship is no more "heterosexual," or even sexual, than the other. And yet, for all the "adult sexuality" they miss and the inadequacies they parade, their relationships are full of feeling, a lost paradise of innocence that, in less charming form, is

118    the temptation of eternal retrogression. They offer a heightened comic understanding of the priorities and evasions of American society and sexual relations, as childhood, extended into middle age, passes into second childhood without so much as a pause or interruption for adulthood. For once, Wilder has found the perfect vehicle and tone for his mixed feelings about America, and there is no covert nastiness or cheap cynicism. The American Dream, male and female versions, with all its materialism and adolescent exuberance, goes through perversion and comes out the other side. And Marilyn, the little girl playing in her mama's falsies, the sex symbol of America, is right there where the dream turns into a cartoon and back into a dream again.

As the gold digger in *Gentlemen Prefer Blondes*—Hawks's considerably reworked version of the Anita Loos play and musical—Marilyn consciously exploits the sex-bomb image that men, with their lascivious glances, have forced on her, and gets her revenge in spades . . . or, rather, diamonds. In this spoof of ooh-la-la, it is not women but men who are exposed and humiliated, and the two girls, strutting their wares, command awe much like two renowned gunfighters. The setting, an ocean liner, is deliberately garish, with pinks and reds clashing unmercifully; and the males, usually seen in groups, consist of a little boy, an old man, a suitor who turns out to be a spy, and a group of athletes so intent on toning up their bodies that they fail to observe Jane Russell in their midst. Here, Marilyn has accepted her image and will go one better: she is determined to get paid for it. In the long run, what makes her attractive to men—to a particular kind of man—will wither, while they turn to younger and younger versions of her. She must, therefore, shore up something for her old age, and diamonds are better security than love or marriage. Russell, the champion of love and marriage, is soon disillusioned and joins Marilyn in common cause. Opting for diamonds over *a* diamond, she dons a blond wig in imitation of Marilyn, in cynical deference to the preference of gentlemen.

Monroe's career, with her death, became a *fait accompli*. It is no longer possible to separate the woman from her image, or to know if it was alterable or not. We can regret all the missed opportunities, but can we wish away the sex "hype" on which Marilyn's career was built and her soul strung out? What if Marilyn had been, as the saying goes, "herself"? Would anyone have gone to the movies to see a sexless and childlike young woman, with dirty-blond hair, a soft voice, ambition, and an inferiority complex? And would we, or she, have been better off if Marilyn had never been born, and if Norma Jeane, sitting on the front porch of some Southern California rest home, or even surrounded by a brood of children, were rocking her way into oblivion? All we can say is that she has told us, through her stardom and abuse, more about ourselves than we would have known without her.

*all the available light*

# FACE VALUE

*Sabrina Barton*

*M*arilyn Monroe manages to take up a lot of space on-screen. Exactly how much space seems to be a matter of some debate, but my point here has nothing to do with actual inches or pounds, and everything to do with the far-reaching effects of her vivid, dynamic, expansive star performance.

Now, I certainly recognize the camera's relentless fascination with Monroe's shapely, shining surfaces; that fascination supplies the gender studies classes that I teach with textbook examples of how Hollywood cinema can fetishize the female body. At the same time, however, the term "fetishize" implies a gaze that reduces the woman to a merely passive object. As far as I'm concerned, the concept of passive "objectness" fails to capture the Marilyn effect.

Monroe actively performs. Most frequently, she performs the role of performer (model, showgirl, musical entertainer) and, consequently, presents a stylized, exaggerated femininity. We witness the powerful and pervasive effects of her performance of femininity as, from movie to movie, Monroe's characters dazzle, dumbfound, and overwhelm male costars. We might even venture to say that Marilyn Monroe represents a form of power: the power of a femininity actively performed.

However, rather than assessing the power of her performed femininity at face value, writers have mostly tried to penetrate Marilyn Monroe's shiny surfaces in order to get to her underlying "truth," a truth that tends to classify her as objectified and/or victimized.

I suspect that it is only now, decades after her heyday, that feminist critics can begin to contemplate the significance of Monroe's performed identity. This is only natural: cultural commentators necessarily tell different stories about our stars at different historical moments according to our differing social, political, and emotional needs.

## MONROE AND FEMINISM

In the early 1960s, what we needed was Betty Friedan (among others) to mobilize feminist discussions of gender and power. Friedan did not overlook cinema's role in shaping cultural conceptions of femininity. In *The Feminine Mystique* (1963), she observed that whereas the classic female star of 1930s and 1940s Hollywood cinema once evoked a "complex individual of fiery temper, inner depth, and a mysterious blend of spirit and sexuality," as exemplified by Greta Garbo, Marlene Dietrich, Bette Davis, and Katharine Hepburn, the female star in the course of the 1950s came to evoke the stereotypical "sexual object, babyface bride, or housewife," and here Friedan mentions Marilyn Monroe, Debbie Reynolds, Brigitte Bardot, and Lucille Ball.[1] In 1974, Molly Haskell's *From Reverence to Rape* asked of the Monroe icon: "What was she, this breathless, blond, supplicating symbol of sexuality . . . ?" and then answered: "She was partly a hypothesis, a pinup fantasy of the other woman as she might be drawn in the marital cartoon fantasies of Maggie and Jiggs, or Blondie and Dagwood. . . ."[2] [Editor's Note: The chapter from which this is quoted appears earlier in this volume.]

Observe how both Haskell and Friedan criticize the *unreality* inherent in Monroe's femininity ("stereotype," "object," "symbol," "hypothesis," "pinup," "fantasy," "cartoon"). In a moment, I will propose a different, more affirmative way of thinking about the unreality of gender.

First, though, let's look briefly at an example of the sort of thing to which Friedan and Haskell were reacting. Twentieth Century-Fox's poster for *How to Marry a Millionaire* (1953) fills its space front-and-center with a seductively beckoning, magenta-satined, heavy-lidded Monroe (costars Lauren Bacall and Betty Grable are reduced to mere head-and-shoulder shots, peering around Monroe's hips). The trailer for *How to Marry a Millionaire* opens with the offer, in garish pink lettering, of a uniquely satisfying cinema spectacle: "Now—To Fill the CinemaScope Screen as Only They Can: Marilyn Monroe, Betty Grable, and Lauren Bacall." Next, a robust male voice-over exults that "Monroe, Grable, and Bacall add their own wonderful dimensions to the eye-filling dimensions of CinemaScope." As each name is pronounced, that actress sweeps into the frame, her so-called "wonderful dimensions" garbed in lavish and spectacular evening dress.

There is no question that *Millionaire*'s trailer confirms everything that the women's movement has found so offensive about mainstream fifties cinema. Women put on display. For male visual pleasure. In overblown productions. Ruled by box-office returns.

There is also no question that such images are made, not born. Marilyn Monroe was scripted, filmed, and packaged by her studio to be a sex object. Led by Gloria Steinem, many feminists soon came to see Monroe as an innocent victim sacrificed on the altar of patriarchy's "unreal" standards for femininity. First in *Ms.* magazine and later in book form, Steinem (as a *Newsweek* blurb on the Signet paperback puts it) "explores the real woman behind the bombshell persona." [Editor's Note: Steinem's extensive analysis of Monroe appears elsewhere in this volume.] The feminist premise: by penetrating Hollywood's false image (the stereotype, the sex object) we pay tribute to the real woman behind the mask, revealing the truth of her humanity, the core of her sensitivity and suffering. Since then, the "real" Norma Jeane has been explored again and again by biographers who offer ever-lengthening lists of her actual, behind-the-scenes traumas: illegitimacy, rape, failed marriages, abortions, spousal battering, sexual dysfunction, panics about physical appearance, and so on.

What gets lost amid all of this probing scrutiny is any means of understanding Monroean performance in its own right. Indeed, perhaps the sheer performativity of Monroe actually incites such excavations, as journalists, critics, novelists, and biographers strive to penetrate Marilyn's façade and pin down her essence.

What might be gained, I'd like to ask, from taking Marilyn Monroe's star persona, her *unreality,* at face value? It seems to me that—at least from the vantage point of our own historical moment—Monroe's star image carries a power and significance that have been obscured by the terms "object" and "victim."

## PERFORMING GENDER

I'm a performer—didn't you know? Songs and dances.
—Monroe in *River of No Return,* 1954

Our psychologically inclined culture tends to regard the performed or performing self as a false front, as something to be penetrated in order to get at the authentic core self. Hollywood cinema itself is full of plots that hang on the question of when the male hero will finally crack a female character's fabricated pose of disinterest (it takes the combined efforts of James Stewart *and* Cary Grant to finally dissolve Katharine Hepburn's icy exterior in *The Philadelphia Story*). The persistent theme of dismantling feminine performance to expose a woman's hidden truth does, I think, raise the question of whether attributing "inner depth" (Friedan's phrase) to a character's self is in every case a positive thing.

Postmodern philosopher Judith Butler has theorized identity as staged rather than innate, as performed rather than expressive of a preexisting core self.[3] Butler recognizes that the acts and costumes and gestures of gendered identity may well produce the *effect* of an internal core, an effect that individuals buy into, but the point remains: we are still talking about a performance, not an essence of self.

The concept of gender identity as performative provides us with a useful lens through which to appreciate the artifice that defines Marilyn Monroe's star image, artifice that has usually been either denigrated or penetrated. Moreover, making the artifice of gender visible through our discussions of Monroe—whether in the media or in the classroom—can help to provide analytical tools for combating a culture that continues to be surprisingly coercive when it comes to dictating what "real" femininity and "real" masculinity are supposed to look like and act like. I am not trying to suggest that Marilyn Monroe herself consciously wielded such tools, nor that 1950s audiences were necessarily in a position to interpret Monroe's image as performative. However, the way we talk about Monroe *now* can encourage an understanding of gender as a look and an act, as a matter of "songs and dances." Such an understanding can provide a more fluid, creative, and forgiving space from which to practice our own day-to-day gender identities.

Monroe performs characters that are thoroughly defined as performative. If, of all her films, *Gentlemen Prefer Blondes* (Howard Hawks, 1953) receives a disproportionate amount of attention, that is perhaps because it so fully and so freely celebrates Marilyn Monroe's sheer powers of performativity. What is thrown into relief is how the Monroean character thereby thwarts efforts (on the part of other characters or on the part of viewers) to discover, diagnose, and define a real woman behind the bombshell persona.

Throughout *Gentlemen Prefer Blondes,* various characters persist in their attempts to uncover the truth of Monroe's Lorelei Lee. It's a losing proposition. When Lorelei Lee parts from her fiancé, Gus Esmond (Tom Noonan) to embark on a cruise to Paris with her best friend Dorothy Shaw (Jane Russell), Lorelei doesn't realize that she is being followed by a private detective, Ernie Malone (Elliot Reid), who has been hired by Gus's millionaire father to acquire evidence that Lorelei is nothing more than a calculating, corrupt gold digger. But in spite of Malone's best efforts to expose Lorelei as a "mercenary nitwit" (Malone's words), he fails to uncover a calculating woman posing behind a mask of naïveté. Behind her "mask" is . . . simply more of the same. And because Lorelei is all on the surface, her male pursuers are baffled in their attempts to "get" her.

This is tricky territory. To characterize Monroe's persona as surfaces all the way down may begin to insinuate superficiality and vacancy. Dumbness (nitwit-ness) remains one of the most controversial features of the Marilyn Monroe persona, and I am certainly not celebrating it as a positive image. Nonetheless, the absence of an inner depth or truth of self, as performed by Monroe through displays of stunning unwittingness, functions very usefully to produce impenetrability. If no one really knows what is going on inside her, that is because her identity can only be accessed at face value.

In the opening of *Gentlemen Prefer Blondes,* the camera catches sight of a gawky Gus as he watches Lorelei perform "Two Little Girls from Little Rock" on stage with Dorothy. Shot/reverse shot editing, conventionally used to subordinate female objects to a male look, turns parodic when we catch sight of the small, bespectacled Gus, cringing before the powerhouse of red-sequined female sexuality exploding on stage. As with Lorelei's showstopping "Diamonds Are a Girl's Best Friend" number later in the movie, it is always Lorelei who controls Gus from the stage, not vice versa. Throughout the movie, Gus is repeatedly pushed to the margins of the frame as

*all the available light*

Lorelei thoroughly invades his space, both physically and emotionally. The two women, by contrast, easily share spaces, and even personas.

The phenomenon of Monroe's performativity in *Gentlemen Prefer Blondes* is especially fascinating for its suggestion that identity may be performed across the surfaces of someone *else's* body. In the climactic courtroom scene, Dorothy "matches" herself to—masquerades as—Lorelei (blond wig, wide eyes, breathy little voice) in order to protect and defend her best friend, who has been accused of stealing a diamond tiara. Called to the stand, Dorothy-performing-Lorelei actively deflects male questioning (and imminent discovery) by seizing control of the courtroom through song and dance. After flirting with police, lawyers, witnesses, and judges, Dorothy finally tosses off her fur coat and launches into a physically aggressive version of Lorelei's signature "Diamonds Are a Girl's Best Friend" number, taking up and taking over the patriarchal spaces of the courtroom.

When Russell-playing-Dorothy plays Monroe-playing-Lorelei, there is a dizzying effect of mask upon mask upon mask. Distinctions among star personae, movie characters, and real selves blur. Indeed, the transgressive promise of this scene has been fulfilled by all of the multiplied images and drag performances of Monroe that continue to challenge the concept of a fixed inner self.

In her disapproving feminist critique of *Gentlemen Prefer Blondes,* Maureen Turim finds it "ironic that in a film about performances, acting is denied in favor of 'matching.'"[4] But this movie is all about the play and playfulness of surfaces, not about actorly uniqueness. Performative identity is impossible to pin down ("You are Lorelei Lee, aren't you?" the judge asks Dorothy anxiously). Immediately following the courtroom scene (which he has just witnessed), Mr. Esmond orders his son Gus to "marry anyone but that monster, Lorelei Lee." At that very moment, though, Gus is attempting to introduce his father to Monroe's (not Russell's) Lorelei Lee, who then offers evidence of her identity by gesturing to a paper-doll cutout display of herself and Dorothy. Overwhelmed and disoriented, Mr. Esmond cries out that there are "thousands of Lorelei Lees coming at me from everywhere!" The patriarch panics as performative feminine surfaces fill the space.

*Gentlemen Prefer Blondes* concludes, as Hollywood tradition dictates, with a wedding scene. However, when Lorelei and Dorothy promenade together down the aisle, perfectly matched in dress and gait, the two grooms seem like little more than bystanders to this performance of victorious femininity. Although admittedly the women are always on display as sexual objects that mirror 1950s fantasies of femininity, at the same time Lorelei and Dorothy also take charge of how that fantasy gets performed and played out. If we, as film viewers, habitually reduce Monroe to a fetishized object, then we fail to see the forms of power she wields. In particular, we overlook her ability to control or elude the agendas of the male characters who (they think) have her snared for their own desires.

The unexpected power of the fantasy woman: this is the paradox explored by director Billy Wilder's *The Seven Year Itch* (1955). When wife and son leave hot New York City for the summer, the film's protagonist, Richard (Tom Ewell), finds his psyche and his apartment quickly invaded by The Girl (as the credits refer to her) who has sublet the apartment upstairs. Initially, Richard appears to be in charge of both spaces. He buzzes the new tenant into the building; then he fantasizes (in the form of a movie-within-the-movie) his planned evening with this woman. We watch as, according to his script, Monroe materializes in an exotic evening dress and quickly melts, succumbing first to his classical piano-playing (Rachmaninoff) and then to his passionate embrace. However, the woman (in fetching pink matador pants) who ultimately joins him fails to follow his script. She prefers a rousing round of "Chopsticks" on the piano, and her profoundest wish is to get herself a good night's sleep by taking up residence in Richard's air-conditioned living room. Later, Monroe's character finds that by pulling up a few floorboard nails, she can conveniently invade his space any time to take advantage of his air-conditioning.

I do not mean to imply that The Girl isn't also functioning as a sexualized object of fantasy. Is she ever. Wilder misses no opportunity to frame her figure in strategically lit silhouettes, and the script is rampant with double entendres about bodies and heat. However, Richard is repeatedly shown to be at the mercy of his larger-than-life fantasy female, not the other way around. Although we hear him boast on the phone that he might just have "Marilyn Monroe" in his apartment, the hero has no clue how to get a handle (much less a hand) on this surfacey rendering of ideal femininity. Moreover, as he loses control over his apartment space, Richard also loses mastery over his mental and physical self: he develops a twitching thumb that betrays his sexual obsession with The Girl.

With its focus as much on Richard's sexual hysteria as on Monroe's sexual allure, *The Seven Year Itch* reveals how the gray-flanneled employee and beleaguered father of the 1950s is driven to use fantasies of idealized women to bolster his own insecure performance of manliness. Richard's wife Helen (Evelyn Keyes), a frequent and sardonic viewer of his fantasy-female "mini-movies," at one point jokes that he's now fantasizing about women in "CinemaScope," "Technicolor" and "Stereophonic sound" (which, of course, he is!). Her comment calls attention to how very intertwined male fantasy and Hollywood cinema are in the matter of generating cultural images of gender.

### Interior Scaffolding

Small wonder that it is the fifties in which Marilyn Monroe becomes a huge star. Hollywood movies and women's bodies had both expanded. Cinerama, 3-D,

CinemaScope, and VistaVision used scale and spectacle to combat the threat that television (and other leisure activities) posed to Hollywood's profit margin. At the same time, the culture's celebration of hyperfemininity helped to combat the threat to traditional gender arrangements posed both by women's recent experience of wartime labor outside the home and by the continued influx of women into the world of nondomestic employment.

The profound concern to restabilize gender difference during the 1950s, and the consequent efforts to direct women into conventionally feminine roles, have been well documented by social historians. Stephanie Coontz, Peter Filene, Elaine Tyler May, and Lynn Spigel have each examined how, following the upheaval of sex roles on the home front during World War II, 1950s public discourses became obsessed with defining and restricting gender.[5]

For critic Maureen Turim, *Gentlemen Prefer Blondes* unabashedly participated in this coercive effort by marketing Marilyn Monroe and Jane Russell as commodities, as the Cadillacs, so to speak, of the silver screen: "It is the hourglass figure, the lush, full body of Fifties fashion which sells the film."[6] At the same time, says Turim, the female stars represent "an exaggerated form of the role assigned to all middle-class women in the Fifties."[7] Turim has also argued that the built-in hourglass shape of the New Look dress itself functioned as a form of gilded bondage, helping to restore postwar women to sexualized, maternal roles.[8] The New Look dress (introduced by Christian Dior in 1947) achieved its peak of American popularity in the early fifties. It is certainly the case that the dress's interior scaffolding[9]—its cinched-in waist and padded, wired, stiffened chest and hips—actively constructed woman's "wonderful dimensions" (as *Millionaire*'s trailer put it). But by the same token, then, those dimensions are revealed—at least to today's audiences—to be a matter of design and fantasy.

There is a provocative paradox at work here: in order to achieve nature's ideal femininity (quite a Victorian project), women would need to go shopping. Restoring natural femininity seemed to depend on commodities. Even as cinema, advertising, popular psychology, fashion magazines, and conduct manuals such as *How to Be a Woman* (1951) loudly proclaimed the truth of women's preexistent or essential femininity, such discourses also incessantly offered or demanded commodified surface "proofs" of that femininity. The conundrum: what is natural and what is cultural? As an *Atlantic Monthly* article from 1950 entitled "Women Aren't Men" laments, inhabitants of America's

> competitive, materialistic world have observed the importance of woman's role as the repository of continuity and purposeful living derived from their biological and social functions. Our technological civilization has atrophied their emotions, and nothing is more horrible than a woman whose instinctive reactions have been destroyed.[10]

Two years later, this article's worst nightmare concerning the "atrophied" results of our "technological civilization" unfolds in the form of the 1952 sex-change operation of Christine Jorgensen. U.S. society and its media, predictably enough, are obsessed with the story. A particularly telling example of the gender tensions that erupted around the Jorgensen case appears in a May 13, 1953, press report from *Variety,* which begins this way:

> Christine Jorgensen may think she looks like Lauren Bacall on a foggy day—but to a flock of newsmen last Thursday morning . . . the recently baked Danish pastry might just as well have been Gorgeous George in drag. When it came to handling "herself" in the clinches of reportorial probing, Christine batted her eyes like an ingenue but showed a steely side that would have turned the scalpels had it been as apparent in Copenhagen as in Los Angeles.[11]

The report uses surface-conscious and appearance-oriented images (Bacall, drag, eye-batting, ingenue) to set up a contrast with the underlying truth of Jorgensen's "steely" innate manliness that by all rights should have "turned the scalpels" in Copenhagen. It is interesting that Bacall rather than Hollywood's biggest star of the time, Monroe, is invoked as an example of authentic femininity. Perhaps comparing Jorgensen to Monroe carried a greater risk of calling attention to gender as a performance, a performance not limited to transsexuals.

After all, the bodily transformation of Jorgensen was not unrelated to the consumer's quest for the exaggerated dimensions promised by the New Look dress. Since the flapper era, shopping had been associated with the economic and sexual power of modernity's New Woman. Monroe's movies frequently show her active pleasure in consumerism. In *How to Marry a Millionaire,* for example, Pola Debevoise's (Monroe) first question to her friend Schatze Page (Bacall), upon learning that she's engaged to a millionaire, is "Have you been shopping yet?" One of my favorite moments in *Gentlemen Prefer Blondes* comes when Dorothy turns to Lorelei in the back of the cab after their Paris shopping spree and declares: "That was fun, wasn't it?" to which Lorelei responds, "Yes! It's the first time I've been shopping without a man along!" I recognize that this is capitalism advertising itself, but the moments also depict female bonding, female autonomy, and female fun.

The association of female consumerism with a potentially transgressive form of autonomous feminine desire was a genuine concern amid the economic boom of a postwar America that both needed and feared the very real power of women shoppers. The film industry faced its own version of this particular dilemma: how to lure women out to the movies while, ideologically, returning them to the home? In a 1953 *Variety* piece, "Women, Bless 'Em, and Why Pix Should Woo 'Em at B.O.,"

Paramount executive producer Jerry Wald warns that "women control seventy percent of the nation's personal wealth" and that "working girls earn $30,000,000,000 per year, enabling them to rock the box office if not the cradle." The opposition of "cradle" to "box office" reveals Wald's ambivalent recognition that fantasy-driven female consumerism might displace woman's maternal and domestic instincts.

From a feminist vantage point, decades later, we can use Marilyn Monroe's image to make visible how postwar beliefs about femininity anxiously tussled between nature and culture, between essence and performance. Again, there is no question that Monroe's "wonderful dimensions"—her particular manner of taking up space—facilitated the star's objectification and victimization by the Hollywood industry. Twentieth Century-Fox tirelessly exploited Monroe's sexualized image, and in 1953 she was voted biggest box-office draw after propelling both *Gentlemen Prefer Blondes* and *How to Marry a Millionaire* into the top-ten money-makers of the year.[12] However, to stop at objectification and victimization in our discussion of Marilyn Monroe would be to allow those two categories themselves to take up all the space in how we understand and interact with her influential cultural legacy. Monroe's power also exists in more positive forms right there, right on the surface. If we have the eyes to see it.

Paying attention to the weak eyesight of Pola Debevoise, Monroe's character in *How to Marry a Millionaire,* may help to focus the question of what we as viewers do or do not see about Monroe and her movies.

The comedy concerns three models who appropriate a fancy uptown apartment and launch their scheme to meet rich men. Pola spends a great deal of time snatching her eyeglasses off her face every time a man walks into the room. However, one safe space to wear glasses turns out to be in the women's restroom of a ritzy restaurant where Pola's glasses quickly come on instead of off. The three friends (who have landed wealthy dinner dates), meet up in the "Powder Room" to exchange notes; in particular, they discuss what Pola's date looks like, since she can't see a thing without her glasses. Then, after Schatze Page and Loco Dempsey (Grable) exit, Pola, still wearing her eyeglasses, crosses to the full-length, four-way mirror.

This moment is associated with one of Marilyn Monroe's most famous publicity stills. You're probably familiar with the image: Monroe wrapped in shiny magenta satin—glasses nowhere in sight—smiles ecstatically toward the camera while striking a pose, her sexualized surfaces lavishly multiplied by four in the adjacent mirror.

But the thing is, this famous image never actually appears in *How to Marry a Millionaire.* Instead, as Pola checks her image in the full-length mirror, she is wearing her rhinestone eyeglasses. Then, when she does turn toward the camera, it is not in order to strike a glamorous pose for us but merely to return her glasses to her purse and move toward the exit—at which point she promptly walks into a wall. The eyeglasses make a difference. As a prop that Pola removes strategically and repeatedly from the male gaze, the glasses are a constant reminder that Monroe is indeed performing idealized femininity for a specific audience. Also, the fact that Pola cannot see well and is constantly embroiled in slapstick situations without her glasses, pokes fun at seamless images of (non-bespectacled) glamour such as the one frozen in the famous publicity still. Although Pola's happy ending in *How to Marry a Millionaire* includes getting to keep her glasses on, our cultural memory of that movie mostly forces her to keep them off.

What we are willing and able to see in any movie is selective and historical. In 1953, Twentieth Century-Fox's publicity shot of Monroe and the four-way mirror excludes the "blot" of the eyeglasses. But decades later, in a university gender studies classroom, Pola's glasses are much-loved, providing rich opportunities for discussing the cultural fashioning of femininity. These discussions are enlivened by the fact that cat-eye glasses have, as a cultural artifact, accrued so many additional layers of meaning, even *glamour,* over the decades.

Reading characters for their performative elements

makes visible the ways in which images of femininity are manipulable through the wearing or not wearing of eyeglasses, for example. Taking (or teaching) Marilyn Monroe at face value also includes taking note of the criteria for what counts as a valued face. Critics have often commented on Monroe's exaggerated facial maneuvers, maneuvers that can be linked to the concept of femininity as a performance. Perhaps less obvious in its performativity (if only because less remarked upon) is the question of racial identity. Consider the excessive whiteness of Monroe's face and image. For instance: Richard of *The Seven Year Itch* buzzes The Girl into his apartment building; she enters, the 1950s Hollywood ideal of white femininity: white skin, platinum hair, white dress, white earrings, white sandals—not to mention the white bread and potato chips in her grocery bag. This woman glows, a perfect (movie) screen for projected fantasy.

Monroe's effortless ability in movies so innocently to invade male space, or date millionaires, or refuse sex, has everything to do with her performance of *white* femininity. In pointing this out, my aim is not to debunk that performance but rather to consider its cultural implications.

Hollywood movies usually do their best to present racial identity as natural. A slight shift of perspective, however, enables us quite easily to recognize all the ways in which Monroe's whiteness is constructed through the

140 "scaffolding" of lighting, makeup, powder, peroxide, costume, diction, gesture, and gait. During Monroe's "Diamonds Are a Girl's Best Friend" number, a frizzy lock of her peroxide-damaged hair protrudes (to the dismay of my more image-conscious students), a blot in the performance of ideal femininity. During that same musical number, Monroe is circled by pink-tutu'd ballerinas whose faces, upon closer inspection, appear to be darkened with stocking masks (the better to highlight our star). Even sets perform race: look closely at the "Powder Room" scene in *Millionaire*. As the women touch up their (already perfectly polished) whiteness with powder, the camera reveals the restroom's decorative motif: a series of dancing, dark-skinned, turbaned figures.

Marilyn Monroe isn't a force of nature; she is a force of culture. It is the project of performativity critique to retrieve identity from the intangibility of the "natural." One can celebrate the palpable energy and exuberance of Monroean performance by taking it at face value— that is, by giving up the search for the poor, objectified victim behind the mask. At the same time, by paying attention to the power lodged in the surfaces of Monroe's performance of culturally admired femaleness, it may become more possible to imagine alternative performances of diverse identities.[13]

Analyzing Marilyn Monroe serves as a means of analyzing an important chapter in the history of what idealized "femininity" means. Movie images rarely interpret themselves. We come to Monroe's legacy, decade after decade, with fresh tools, desires, and agendas, thereby edging the familiar material into ever-new interpretive frameworks. Stories about objectified and victimized women continue to have an important place in the history of patriarchal culture. But cultural meanings are multiple, fluid, and ever-changing. So, too, will be the ways in which we see our stars.

# SEXY AND HER SISTERS

*Lore Segal*

"Always one pert and pretty and always one with glasses," wrote the poet Dylan Thomas noting the curious tendency of girls to come in pairs—the one you looked at, and the other one.

I have a confession to make: the one I had trouble looking at was Marilyn Monroe. It's a matter of taste. I like my fruit sour, drink my coffee bitter, and wear muted and heathered colors. Marilyn made me blink. She was too white and pink and gold for me. And I never understood the way she put a song over. Don't tell anybody, but it reminded me of the way preschoolers learn to illustrate every phrase of every song with an appropriate gesture. Then there was that thing she did with her mouth, which, it seemed to me, ought to have been hidden inside the darkness of somebody else's mouth. I was embarrassed for her.

Because I didn't look *at* Marilyn Monroe but always a little to the right, a little to the left, of her, I came to be interested in the Other One. The Other Ones. What are the roles played by other women in Marilyn Monroe movies?

There are the production numbers that back Marilyn with a chorus, a whole screenful of pretty women. *Gentlemen Prefer Blondes* partners her with one, and *How to Marry a Millionaire* with two fellow bombshells. And there are the movies that share Dylan Thomas's insight and pair pertest, prettiest Marilyn with a sidekick with metaphorical glasses. Remember the good-natured, horse-faced waitress in *Bus Stop,* the softhearted, self-deprecating divorcée in *The Misfits.* What about the sympathetic roommate in *Let's Make Love*? You can't remember anything about her? You weren't meant to. Sidekick serves as Marilyn's Horatio—the friend who is always conveniently at hand to have a heart-to-heart with. It is to Sidekick that the Marilyn character reveals her fears and her dreams for the future. We overhear what she is saying and learn everything the plot needs us to know about her. They are good souls, these sidekicks. They root for Marilyn. They look out for her. Sidekick may have problems in her own life, but we are not invited to care. We forget her even when she is on screen. She has her being to the right or

*all the available light*

left of the attention that highlights and haloes Marilyn Monroe. Partially eclipsed, Divorcée peers over Marilyn's shoulder in order to catch the crumbs from the conversation that Clark Gable, and a second handsome male—that a whole crew of males, some handsome, some not—are addressing to Marilyn. When the plot needs to be rid of her, Divorcée catches sight of her ex and his new wife and off she goes to look after *them*.

The trouble is that Hollywood has trouble looking at plain girls. They spoil your screen. The girls who *play* plain would, in most of life's contexts, be great-looking women. Think of Eve Arden and how much of her on-screen life she spent making wry jokes about the difficulty of getting a man—he didn't have to be handsome. And the movies cannot stomach the Girl with the Glasses—here I'm talking about literal glasses. "Girls who wear spectacles seldom get their necks tickled" went the tag Marilyn misquotes in *How to Marry a Millionaire.* Everybody knows that this recurring girl wears glasses not to compensate for her bad vision but so as to remove them from her nose at Handsome Male's request. She takes off her glasses, lets down her hair, and turns into—or turns out to have been all along—Pert and Pretty herself!

This is Hollywood's version of an ancient human dream on which the Grimm fairy tales and the cosmetics industry agree: inside every homely girl there's a beauty waiting to be invited to the party. Love performs the makeover. Cinderella wipes the workaday ashes from her face, slips on the magical gown, and gate-crashes the ball. I, the audience, am Cinderella. My ordinariness, my shyness, my bad eyesight never were the true me. Look! The prince sees me! The two ugly sisters don't even recognize that this is me! Everybody has stopped dancing to gawk for I'm not only beautiful but, mirror, mirror on the wall, the most beautiful of all, the most beautiful in the room, in the whole country, worldwide! Isn't it wonderful to think that Marilyn Monroe lived this scenario every time she walked through a door?

THERE ARE TWO central myths about womankind that have something to say about the relation of beauty to virtue. One says that a beautiful woman is, like her mother Eve, the source of Evil: *Niagara* casts Marilyn as an adulteress who conspires to kill her husband, and *Don't Bother to Knock* tries to make Marilyn out to be a murderous sociopath.

The other myth, exemplified in the *Cinderella* story, says that Beauty equals Goodness. Cinderella is as good as she is beautiful—a hard worker, friend to animals, modest, patient under oppression. As a reward, she gets the Handsome Prince. The Ugly Sisters are lazy, cruel, and vain. Bad is tantamount to Ugly. (The movies, like the kids in a schoolyard, believe that fatsos, string beans, shrimps, and four-eyes deserve to be teased and tormented. They never get invited to that ball.)

Marilyn's mature comedies trust us to have internalized both myths so that our expectations can be both laughed at and satisfied. In *Let's Make Love*, sexy Marilyn is sweet and nice and good. She sympathetically coaches the newest member of the cast who has been hired because he looks like the millionaire the play is going to make fun of. It is lucky for the plot that her innocent decency keeps her from catching on to the fraud: her protégé is the *actual* millionaire hanging around to make love to her.

*There's No Business Like Show Business* casts Marilyn Monroe in a supporting role usually reserved for a Bad Sister: she plays the hard-nosed, ambitious actress who throws her weight around. In the end, when it's Pert and Pretty who gets the lead and gets the guy, old Hardnose is supposed to slam out of the theater. Interesting that Marilyn plays the stereotypical good and stereotypical bad role as one role.

The two hilarious husband-hunting comedies, too, tweak both myths by conflating the bad girl and the good girl—the sexy gold digger and the girl with a heart—into the one and only Marilyn. It is the neatest trick. *Gentlemen Prefer Blondes* casts Jane Russell as a *comparatively* good girl, I guess: *she,* at least, insists that her men be handsome, unlike her friend Marilyn, who makes out with the funny, fat, bald old man because he has access to his ugly, snooty old wife's jewelry. The movie has a musical number that provides a mitigating circumstance: who are we to deny these gorgeous girls from the wrong side of the tracks the right to compensate themselves with diamonds? So who would have thought that Marilyn has, all along, really loved the nerd with the glasses and the rich father, and that he has loved her all along?

And *How to Marry a Millionaire* tweaks every convention around the girl with the glasses. It's Marilyn who wears them and when she takes them off, she's blind as a bat and presumably cannot see that the millionaire she marries is one of the Shrimps. The sympathetic attraction between them is that he's blind as a bat too, as well as terminally shortsighted in his money matters.

I don't think that we have here an example of Hollywood's meditation on the mixed nature of good and evil. It is a dream that, arguably, we no longer dream in the year 2002. These movies satisfy a desire that Cinderella might be as virtuous as she was sexy, like Rita Hayworth's *Gilda,* who, after a virtual striptease, turns up in a white blouse with an old-fashioned bow tied under the chin. In that dreadful movie *The Prince and the Showgirl,* and in the wonderful *The Seven Year Itch,* Marilyn makes love without making it. Is it the male dream that the most voluptuous, the sexiest, the lovingest girl is extravirgin chaste? The broad after whom every man leches is, has always been, and will forever remain a good girl.

Finally, does our wish project upon her—or was there in Marilyn Monroe's person—a sweetness that disabled the myth of the bitch and the cat? Not one of that trainful of Pert and Pretties in *Some Like It Hot* was cast as cross or mean or sneaky. The sidekicks—the girls with the metaphorical glasses—are, one and all, good-hearted girls who care about Marilyn. What became of the narrative convention that out of any two beauties one will be Cinderella and the other a sister with an ugly heart who rivals Cinderella for the spotlight and the prince? Marilyn and her fellow bombshells lie, cheat, charm, fall in love, and get rich together in harmonious, hilarious sisterhood. There are, in Marilyn's major movies, no Ugly Sisters.

A POSTSCRIPT:

I've said that Marilyn Monroe was not my cup of tea, so it's irritating to recollect the indelible impression of seeing her in person at a summer stock performance in Connecticut. The play was by the late Ettore Rella and concerned an interracial love affair in the modern mode and in blank verse. The only surviving member of my circle of friends from that period has helped me reconstruct the situation. Ettore and his wife Jessie knew Arthur Miller. This was in the days when the affair was still sub rosa. Marilyn spent time with the Rellas. Legend says that she had a yearning for the intellectual. The Rellas reported that she was eager, bright, and very nice.

Ettore and Jessie lived in a small Manhattan walk-up on West 14th Street. The ceilings were high. I have a memory of dark velvets. One of the rooms was dedicated to a puppet theater. My friend has sent me a snapshot showing herself and her late husband, the Rellas, a couple I don't recognize, and Marilyn Monroe laughing into the camera. Marilyn wears white and appears to be the source of light. On the border, written in ink, it says, "Christmas 1956." I'm miffed that I'm not at that party.

My own sighting of Marilyn Monroe in Connecticut must have been the subsequent summer. It was an open-air performance, during the intermission. We were not an autograph-hunting crowd and wouldn't be caught dead standing around a movie star and gawking. We gawked and continued walking. In my memory, Marilyn Monroe stands alone surrounded by a space. Her weight is on the left foot. She wears a slim skirt with a remarkable slit up one side and a light, white blouse open at the throat. Her hair is short and easy, her expression complicated—self-conscious and shy, pleased and patient under the assault of our eyes.

## THE PRINCE AND THE SHOWGIRL

*Sir Laurence Olivier*

*T*he first word came to Cecil Tennant from Warners, I think, that Marilyn Monroe's company, run by Milton Greene, her stills photographer, would be very interested in filming *The Sleeping Prince,* and that she would like me to produce and direct her in it. So Terry Rattigan, Cecil, and I buzzed over to New York for the great meeting. We called on her in her apartment on Sutton Place for some jubilant conviviality.

There were two entirely unrelated sides to Marilyn. You would not be far out if you described her as a schizoid; the two people that she was could hardly have been more different. Her three visitors on this first meeting were a little the worse for wear by the time she vouchsafed her presence, as she had kept us waiting an hour, ably and liberally refreshing ourselves at the assiduous hands of Milton Greene. Eventually, I went boldly to her door and said, "Marilyn, for the love of God, come in to us. We're dying of anxiety!" She came in. She had us all on the floor at her feet in a second. I have no memory of a single word that was uttered, except that all was as convivial and jubilant as could be.

The evening wore on to its self-congratulatory close; we were all making our departure when Marilyn, in the small voice she sometimes used to good effect, gently piped: "Just a minute. Shouldn't somebody say something about an agreement?" By George, the girl was right; we arranged for a purely business meeting in the morning, and I was then to take her to lunch at the "21" Club.

By the end of the day, one thing was clear to me: I was going to fall most shatteringly in love with Marilyn, and *what* was going to happen? There was no question about it, it was inescapable, or so I thought; she was so adorable, so witty, such incredible fun and more physically attractive than anyone I could have imagined, apart from herself on the screen. I went home like a lamb reprieved from the slaughter just for now, but next time. . . . Wow! For the first time now it threatened to be "poor Vivien"! (Almost twenty years earlier, it had been "poor Jill.")[1]

Vivien was really very sweet about being passed over for the role she had created, considering that in telling her I had chosen to be clumsily truculent. After all, it *was* her part, even if she did know that she had not been wildly successful in it at the Phoenix, and that the dazzling heights of fame that Marilyn had achieved were unchallengeable. But that is something that is never easy to accept, and she behaved with attractive understanding and shrugged it all off beautifully. I was grateful and relieved to find no cause for anxiety in that area.

The day of the great arrival dawned, and Marilyn was wafted onto this blessed plot in the illustrious charge of her new husband, Arthur Miller, a playwright both respected and popular; and so we were under starter's orders. I had arranged that we should have two weeks or so of rehearsals before starting the cameras rolling, so that strangenesses could wear off and we should all feel at home with each other. So many years at the job made it hard to believe that this might be impossible, but, by God, it was.

We started off with two days of press conferences. I had said last thing the night before, being already disturbed, that her famous reputation for unpunctuality somewhat belied the strict professionalism that I seemed to discern in the technique supporting her dazzling spontaneity. It sent up a host of question marks about the as-yet-undiscovered complexities of her psychological makeup. She had been pretty good at the huge press conference in New York, during which, making a gesture, her shoulder strap had broken, and one and all took it to be a gag. Now I said, "Marilyn, dear. Please, pretty please, we cannot be late tomorrow, we *cannot*. The press will take it very unkindly and half of them will be expecting it, so do me a favor and disappoint them, *please*."

She promised, and was one whole hour late. I don't think I've ever been so embarrassed. I filled in as best I could, answering personal questions about myself. My attitude to the giving of interviews was well known, so they had me where they wanted me for once; but interest was petering out a bit by the time she showed up. For the first twenty minutes, all the questions started: "Why are you late?" The way she handled this difficult situation was an object lesson in charm, and in no time at all she had got this vast ballroomful of people nestling cozily in the hollow of her hand. To give her a chance, I spontaneously declared that since many of the questions could not be heard by more than a very few, I would take the liberty of repeating each question, thus making her answers more intelligible (and incidentally gaining for Marilyn a few more seconds to think out the answer).

She would always do exactly what was asked of her by any stills photographer. I marveled at first at this show of discipline and thought it augured well; my reaction only a few weeks later would have been: "Well, of course—she's a model." I think that wherever she gleaned that particular training, it taught her more about

*all the available light*

154 acting than did Lee Strasberg; my opinion of his school is that it did more harm than good to his students and that his influence on the American theatre was misapplied. Deliberately antitechnical, his Method offered instead an all-consuming passion for reality, and if you did not feel attuned to exactly the right images that would make you believe that you were actually *it* and *it* was actually going on, you might as well forget about the scene altogether. Our young American actors felt an aching void where there should have been some training or grounding from which they could leap or fly. In the ten years since the war, there had been very little repertory training; Stanislavsky, upon whose philosophy Strasberg's Actors Studio was founded, was much in the mode in England at the time when we were in Rep in the 1920s. It was a gift we could take advantage of but should not be obsessed by.

I went along to Strasberg's Studio on two occasions early in 1958, when *The Entertainer* was on in New York. On each occasion, his judgments lengthened into a homily which, absolutely off the cuff as it was, mounted into an outpouring of spontaneous wise saws, all unthought out and probably unexpressed before, and therefore dangerously unreliable as information. But he was off, mounting into the skies of his own sudden visions. He was the revivalist minister of pure naturalism. The phrase "natural behaviorism" would have a different meaning dialectically and, to some of us, would lend that redeeming mite more technicality.

He was giving an unduly severe stream of criticism to one young man, who seemed to me to have some sort of natural gift, and at the end of the session I ventured to say as much. Obviously only used to obsequious adulation, Strasberg waved me aside as an ignoramus, saying, "Aw, naw-naw-naw, he has many problems." More gently, I put it to him that removing any shred of confidence the boy might have wasn't likely to help many of them. "Aw, naw-naw-naw."

ONLY A VERY little time before the picture started was I told that Lee Strasberg's wife, Paula, "always came along with Marilyn." This alarmed me considerably, as I had rarely found that coaches were helpful. Philosophically, I clung to the thought, "Oh, well, perhaps she may bring out the better of those two halves." Marilyn was not used to rehearsing and obviously had no taste for it. She proclaimed this by her appearance—hair pulled back under a scarf, bad skin with no makeup, very dark glasses, and an overly subdued manner, which I failed dismally to find the means to enliven. I just prayed that that miracle between the lens and the celluloid would happen for me, as I knew very well it must have done for half a dozen of my colleagues on the West Coast. I managed to contact two of them, Billy Wilder and Josh Logan; they commiserated with me cheerfully (their labors over) and said yes, it was hell, but that I would be getting a pleasant surprise when it was all over. When

Paula arrived, I called off rehearsals for two days in order to go over and over the part, teaching *her* the way of it so that she could then teach Marilyn. Pride was a luxury I couldn't afford. Paula seemed willing to cooperate with every scrap of timing and whatever inflections or stress she thought Marilyn could cope with, "and make her feel it was her idea—you know what I mean?"

The truth came to light with uncanny speed: Paula knew nothing; she was no actress, no director, no teacher, no advisor—except in Marilyn's eyes, for she had one talent: she could butter Marilyn up. On one car journey, I heard Paula play an innings in this, her special ploy, which pinned my ears back as I sat in the front with the two of them in the back. "My dear, you really must recognize your own potential; you haven't even yet any idea of the importance of your position in the world. You are the greatest sex symbol in human memory. Everybody knows and recognizes that, and you should, too. It's a duty which you owe to yourself and to the world; it's ungrateful not to accept it. You are the greatest woman of your time, the greatest human being of your time; of any time, you name it. You can't think of anybody, I mean—no, not even Jesus—except you're more popular." Incredible as that must seem, it is no exaggeration; and it went on in unremitting supply for a good hour, with Marilyn swallowing every word.

This was Paula's unique gift to the art of acting, or rather the artful success of Marilyn's career, out of which the Strasbergs stood to make much capital. This was what, I realized in growing alarm, I was stuck with.

Nevertheless, I refused to treat Marilyn as a special case—I had too much pride in my trade—and would at all times treat her as a grown-up artist of merit, which in a sense she was. Her manner to me got steadily ruder and more insolent; whenever I patiently labored to make her understand an indication for some reading, business, or timing, she would listen with ill-disguised impatience, and when I had finished would turn to Paula and petulantly demand, "Wasseee mean?" A very short way into the filming, my humiliation had reached depths I would not have believed possible.

There was one relief from it: during the coronation sequence, there was no dialogue except what was laid onto the effects sound track later; and so there was no need to go into long explanations before each take, and I could risk side-of-camera directions. To my intense relief, she accepted these like a lamb. "Do a little curtsy as the King passes. Watch for when Dickie Wattis bows by your side, and I'll say when to rise. Now try to look up to your right where the altar is; now look back questioningly at Dickie. He'll hand you an open prayer book for you to follow. Now look up and try to find the Regent towards the altar, find him, but of course he won't look at you, so, a wee bit disappointed, follow in the prayerbook a little while, feel moved by the music." I had a massive selection of records, but she would have nothing but the "Londonderry Air," which had perforce to go on for the whole day. The poor unit nearly went round the bend with it. "Now, catch sight of that stained-glass window—it's the most beautiful picture you can imagine. Let some tears well into your eyes, Marilyn. . . ."

As if by magic, submissive and scrupulously obedient, she followed every instruction exactly and at once and, what is most important, quite perfectly. I had cause to reflect once more, this time with gratitude, "Of course, she's a model."

I had run a closed set, admitting no one who was not actually involved in the work, nobody that was even related to anyone of the press, sad to say thereby making enemies of many whom I had thought of as my friends in that profession. But the press of the entire world was screaming and tearing to get in; the set would have been a shambles. Besides these practical reasons, I had some more theoretical convictions of my own.

I had taken note of the fact that a few weeks after her wedding to Prince Rainier, Princess Grace (Kelly) was presented in a film production of Molnar's *The Swan*. There seemed to be no reason in the world why this should not have been a prodigious box-office success— unless one takes into consideration the fact that for months before her wedding the wealth of romance that surrounded this event ensured that her picture, together with some story or anecdote, would appear in almost every newspaper that could be bought. I believe the public was surfeited with the sight of her name in print, even with her beautiful features and, I am afraid, with her story—in fact, anything that could be associated with her for some little time to come.

This taught me to be wary about Marilyn's promotion. If success has a limit, then so has the publicity which, it is claimed, brings it about. This thought prompted me to soft-pedal. But in spite of the most elaborate precautions, there were leaks galore, all to do with the unhappy atmosphere on the set, with wildly exaggerated tales of screaming rows, *faute de mieux*. Our journalists did not lack for invention.

In the last shooting days, I was allowed one petty triumph in the Prince's first saunter down the chorus line backstage. It was fixed that Marilyn's shoulder strap should break as she made her first curtsy, to echo our first big press call in New York. It was fine, but Marilyn took it into her head that her breast had showed itself. "Nooooh, Marilyn. Nooooh," I said, and called in the boys on the rails as witnesses. The message came back: "They say they weren't looking at Miss Monroe; they were watching Sir Laurence." Knowing as I did the intensity of their appraising curiosity for the first few days of the work, this complete lack of interest was an object lesson in something or other.

The last word on Marilyn belongs to Irina Baronova, Cecil's wife, who had been watching quietly with her

*all the available light*

160 Russian intuitiveness from the darkness off the set: "She has a quite unconscious but basic resistance to acting. She loves to show herself, loves to be a star, loves all the success side of it. But to be an actress is something she does not want at all. They were wrong to try to make one of her. Her wit, her adorable charm, her sex appeal, her bewitching personality—are all part of *her,* not necessarily to be associated with any art or talent."

AFTER THE SCRIPT had all been shot, I had feelings of vague disquiet. As a producer, I was entirely satisfied with the picture, which was to be called *The Prince and the Showgirl;* as an actor, shamelessly unashamed of myself; but as a director, I wished I had got better stuff out of Marilyn. Other directors had, and it lay uneasily on my conscience that I had not. I began to admit to myself that I had not achieved greater perfection because I had shirked the probability of more rows. I asked Marilyn to see the picture run and to bring her husband, Arthur Miller, with her, after which would they please come and talk with me? They agreed and I talked with them sincerely and frankly. If she and Arthur found that they were entirely satisfied, then, God knows, I would be only too happy to leave it at that. They both agreed there was room for improvement, but what could be done now it was over? I told them that if Marilyn would undertake to contribute to a better atmosphere between us, discipline herself to absolute punctuality, accept my word when I passed something as OK and not insist on take after take more than was necessary, I would be willing to reshoot certain scenes. I would guarantee to get the work done in two days, but in no circumstances would I undertake more to help Marilyn. For once I had the other side by the short and curlies, and they knew they had to agree.

The first morning made my heart sink, a sensation I was getting profoundly sick of; we had spent the whole time trying to inject a scintillating spirit into the scene of our first meeting. I had never dreamed up such a variety of expressions, examples, illustrations, images to help inspire the essential wit and sparkle needed to make a lively start to a picture from which a great deal would be expected. Marilyn made her inevitable way towards Paula, who said, "Honey, just think of Coca-Cola and Frankie Sinatra!" I suppose that might have been the Actors Studio approach. God! Don't tell me they would have been right and I wrong throughout this whole thing? Needless to say, it worked; enough to make a man cut his throat, enough for this man, anyway.

The day of the great farewell dawned. It had been agreed that whatever our personal feelings might be, a great act must be put on at the airport; our own crews were careful to take the right pictures of the right-looking embraces which assumed the right intensity of passion for any two great lovers of history: Marilyn and me

*all the available light*

kissing, Vivien and Arthur kissing, Vivien and Marilyn kissing, me and Arthur kissing—it deceived no one. An absurd show, the press called it; who did we think we were kidding? *L'envoi.*

Going home, I thought of all the excitement when the first news of the approaching partnership broke; how Josh Logan had declared it "the most exciting combination since black and white." I thought incredulously of our first meeting and how I had feared falling in love with her. Some weeks later, I had to go across the water to show the film to Jack Warner. Milton Greene grabbed hold of me and said, "How 'bout a stills session tomorrow, huh?"

"By myself?"

"Oh no, with Marilyn, of course."

"*Oh no,* Milton, *no, no, no;* you'll not get me with that dame again!"

"Oh, hell, she won't be that way t'morrow, you'll see. You won't recognize her. She'll be marvelous like she used to be. Besides, we want the picture t'make money, don' we? We've had no promotion at all."

It was as he said; he provided delicious caviar sandwiches, drinks of all kinds, the lushest music. He knew how to lay it on; after all, he'd managed to persuade Marilyn to sign up with him and form their own company—strictly business: his own wife was extremely attractive and intelligent.

Two years or so ago, a couple of my Hollywood friends,

as a sort of joke after a dinner party, ran this now-twenty-five-year-old picture for me on their library projection machine. I was a bit embarrassed, as I didn't know how long it might be before the joke would begin to get a bit tired. However, the picture ran through, much to my surprise. At the finish, everyone was clamorous in their praises; how such enchantment could have been poorly received defied imagination. I was as good as could be, and Marilyn! Marilyn was quite wonderful, the best of all. So.

What do you know?

*all the available light*

# personal geography: marilyn in culture

She was as American as apple pie, or so Catherine Texier would tell us, in "French Kiss," which compares Monroe's style to that of actresses in Texier's native France. In Texier's view, Monroe's relationship to her own sexuality was often expressed as a parody or caricature that would be unthinkable for the French actresses who were her contemporaries. The reasons for this, Texier asserts, are deeply ingrained in both the American soul and the culture that fostered it.

In "Marilyn at the *Mikvah*," novelist Evan Zimroth (whose 1995 book *Gangsters* won the National Jewish Book Award in 1996) charts the almost entirely ignored spiritual journey that Monroe undertook upon her marriage to Arthur Miller: her conversion to Judaism. Why did Monroe embrace her husband's faith even when there was no particular pressure for her to do so? And more important, why did she continue to adhere to it, even when the marriage to Miller ended? For Zimroth, the answers to these questions lie somewhere in the complex and fragrant cauldron of Jewish culture.

Scholar and film historian Dennis Grunes limns another aspect of the cultural Marilyn. By comparing and contrasting her to another popular actress of her day, Audrey Hepburn, Grunes makes the case that Monroe (like Hepburn) is a distinctly postwar phenomenon. According to Grunes, the voluptuous blonde and the ectomorphic brunette are "polar opposites" who somehow manage to exist "back to back" in the continuum of American culture.

## FRENCH KISS
*Catherine Texier*

*W*hen I was a little girl, in the fifties, in France, my beautiful and wild and unstable mother was what I might describe now, in retrospect, as a Marilyn Monroe type. Her low-cut dresses revealed the milky globes of her breasts, which were imposing and fleshy (if not quite as fleshy as those of Marilyn), a wide cloth belt cinched her slender waist, her tight-fitting skirt molded her butt and thighs, with the slit at back falling perfectly between the two straight seams of her panty hose. I remember her, teetering on her stiletto heels, one man or another leaning over her naked shoulders. Her bleached-blond hair was waving in soft, short curls around her face. She even sometimes penciled a mole near her mouth, although I don't know if it was in imitation of Marilyn. I had never heard of the American star at the time, but I knew that the image of saucy, overtly sexy femininity was provocative and deemed totally inappropriate for a mother and a well-behaved young woman. But then my mother was a single mother, and she flaunted her sexuality as a badge of liberation from her father. That look, that persona, the sexpot, the tarty girl, as taken up by the girls of the bourgeoisie, was not a sign of oppression; it was a sign of rebellion.

In spite of her cinched waist, low-cut blouses, and giddy laugh, though, my mother was typically French. Even when she occasionally pushed the boundaries of good taste and good behavior, even when she was a little too sexy, a little too tarty, there was an implicit suggestion that a woman's essential seduction—and by that I mean a woman's attitude, the clothes she wore, the way she spoke and carried herself—was about offering herself to men rather than taking them over.

So I was really surprised when I first watched Marilyn Monroe's movies, which was much later, after I had moved to New York. Her voluptuous curves bursting out of skin-tight dresses, her little girl's voice, her comic wriggling and bouncing, all of that suggested a femaleness exaggerated to the point of a cartoon. This is not what I would have expected from a sex symbol. Marilyn's type of seduction was so over-the-top it came across as manufactured and aggressive, almost a parody.

In *Some Like It Hot,* the confluence between the sex symbol and the parody is particularly obvious. Here are Jack Lemmon and Tony Curtis in drag, shot from the back, hilariously wriggling their behinds in their tight skirts and stroking their tits and teetering on their high-heels and making sure the seams of their panty hose are straight. And moments later, here comes Marilyn, doing the exact same thing! And just as hilariously! Except that her pale skin has this amazing luminosity, her face this extraordinary loveliness, and she's a woman, of course. The underlying idea seemed to be that a woman's sexuality was both arousing and embarrassing—if not downright ridiculous in the way that schoolboys giggle at the sight of a woman partially undressed in sexy, revealing lingerie, to defuse her power, make it less threatening, and so assuage their guilt.

Why? Why was the most powerful American sex symbol—presumably the American male's ultimate fantasy—both a gorgeously sexy woman and a laughable caricature of femininity? And was there something unmistakably, crucially American in that conflicted fantasy? Was Marilyn the expression of American men's profound ambivalence toward women?

The French movie stars who dominated the screen when I was growing up were Catherine Deneuve, Jeanne Moreau, Brigitte Bardot, and, closer to my gen-

*all the available light*

eration, Isabelle Huppert. All of them, even Bardot, the child-woman with the pout, the animal mane and the gorgeous body, emanate a seductive and mysterious femininity, subtly, suggestively offered. It is unthinkable that any of them would be a comedian, or would flaunt her female charms in such an obvious and aggressive way.

One explanation is that sex, in Mediterranean cultures, is a powerful force, to be taken seriously, even revered. Men are the pursuers, the dominant partners, the ones who will unleash the power of women's sensuality. On the other hand, women's power lies in their mysterious and dangerous ability to arouse men's desire. Such is women's power that they need to keep their femininity discreet and understated. French and, in general, Mediterranean women, even if they are exquisitely and sexily put together, learn from an early age to keep their seduction suggestive rather than obvious. If they get too dolled up, if they exhibit too much skin, if they make too much of a show, they'll arouse men too openly and too fast and put themselves at risk, if not create havoc in society in general. The assumption is that Mediterranean men are ticking time bombs, ready to explode at the slightest provocation. In contrast, American men—raised in a more sexually repressed and self-controlled culture—would seem to have a higher arousal point, and need a heavier show of femininity to get going.

Marilyn Monroe started out as a pinup, a calendar girl, posing for cheesecake photos of the kind good

American soldiers pinned in their barracks during World War II and the Korean War. At one point, she went to Korea to sustain the U.S. troops' morale. The pinup was not an image of subtle, unattainable femininity. She was exhibited femininity: exaggerated tits and ass, exaggerated poses short of soft porn. If her image was so suggestive, it's because she had an important role to play. Pinups helped lift the troops' spirits by offering the GIs a moral and sanitary alternative to repeated visits to the local hookers. Marilyn was, in a way, an incarnation of the pinup ideal: a living, breathing, singing, dancing, dumb blonde. A living Barbie doll. The fantasy of soldiers or grown-up men who were still giggly and repressed schoolboys at heart.

Then there was the voice, that little girl's voice, pealing out of that grown-up, female body! So sweet it makes you melt. That breathy, throaty, sugary, whispery voice, a caricature itself of femaleness. And the body itself, with its soft, fleshy tits, the pillowy ass and curvy hips! Even in her full-blown Marilyn Monroe phase, Madonna, buff and cut, with her six-pack abs, didn't get her right. Marilyn's sexiness is in her voluptuous roundness, her total lack of angularity. Marilyn with rippled biceps, Marilyn working out at the gym is unthinkable. The famous numbers: "Diamonds Are a Girl's Best Friend" in *Gentlemen Prefer Blondes*—with Marilyn in a hot-pink dress, long gloves, diamond choker, and a huge bow on her backside, her big eyes so wide open, her luscious mouth pursed into an ever-ready pout—or "My name is Lolita and I am not supposed to play with boys; my heart belongs to Daddy," where Marilyn slides down a pole, wearing black panty hose and a thick sweater in the opening of *Let's Make Love*—all embody the bounciness, voluptuousness, and sheer, juicy lusciousness of the star.

And the part she plays, always the same, almost a burlesque! The bombshell, the dumb blonde, the naïve showgirl looking to marry a millionaire, the gold-digger, but so vulnerable and so innocent and, yes, dumb, that you cannot help loving her. When Marilyn waters a geranium with a cocktail shaker and accidentally drops the pot on the terrace of the married man below, when she falls for Tony Curtis, the fake millionaire with the phony accent and the pretend impotence in *Some Like It Hot,* the joke's supposed to be on her. She does the dumb blonde to perfection. At the same time, even though she plays her straight, there's always an edge of self-parody in her swaying and jiggling and teetering and breathlessness. Hear her say in her little-girl's faux-naïf, high-pitched voice: "There I was with a perfectly strange plumber and no polish on my toenails" in *The Seven Year Itch.* Look at her opening her eyes wide in mock astonishment. It's as if she were saying to the audience, with a wink, "I am not the dumb blonde, I am sending her up."

Yet, Marilyn's vulnerability, her raw sexual power, always transcend the jokes. She dominates the screen in every scene of every movie. The luminosity of her skin and her vitality make her the irresistible center of attraction. Her leading men, in contrast, recede. Tony Curtis in *Some Like It Hot,* Clark Gable and Montgomery Clift in *The Misfits,* Yves Montand in *Let's Make Love,* Laurence Olivier in *The Prince and the Showgirl*—all major stars, brilliant actors, and sex symbols in their own right—are overpowered by her.

Look at Marilyn seducing Tony Curtis in that famous scene in *Some Like It Hot* in which he pretends to be impotent and she offers to "cure" him. Watch her lean on top of him, her formidable breasts, earlier floating miraculously in the sheer sequined dress, now heavily hanging over him, her round arms enveloping his head, telling him, "Relax, don't fight it." Sugar Kane is no Cinderella, and even less Snow White brought back to life by Prince Charming's kisses. The fairy tale has been reversed. It is Tony Curtis, the so-called impotent, insecure male, who yearns to be sexually awoken and aroused by Sugar Kane's voluptuous kisses. Tom Ewell, the nerdy husband in the throes of the seven-year itch, is another American male sorely in need of a sexual cure. We find him poring over a manuscript with a chapter entitled "The Repressed Urge in the Middle-Aged Male" and entertaining delirious fantasies of being overwhelmed by a big-chested woman who aggressively seduces him, until he tries his hand—unsuccessfully—on his gorgeous neighbor.

*The Misfits,* Monroe's last film, finally realizes the fantasy—for real, not for laughs. There, Marilyn at her most heartbreaking, her most vulnerable, her most lovely, not just teetering but practically sleepwalking and stumbling through her scenes, her pale skin rendered even more luminous by the black-and-white photography, still manages to reduce her male leading men to lusting, panting, and weak-at-the-knees little boys. *The Misfits* is a kind of American counterpart to Truffaut's *Jules and Jim* (which, coincidentally, was released the same year, 1961). In *Jules and Jim,* Jeanne Moreau dominates the screen, too, but her feminine presence is more subtle, even androgynous at times, and the balance with her two male leads is more even. Neither Oskar Werner nor Henri Serre is a major star, and they both play sensitive, intellectual men. But they manage to hold their own in front of elusive and mysterious Moreau. They are the ones who will endure after she self-destructs in a suicidal car accident. *The Misfits'* dynamic is radically different. Clift and Gable are supposed to be tough cowboys, virile men whose job is to catch wild mustangs and tame them. In fact, they are primitive boys awed by a sex goddess. When Marilyn finally chooses Clark Gable, he is the one who seems to surrender, lying down, again, letting her take him over. And at the end of the film, although he proves his manhood by catching the wild mustang, he has to release it in order to have her, and it's clear she is the one who's tamed him, not the other way around.

In Europe, the cliché about America is that it is the

women who are in charge, while men let themselves be dominated. Marilyn Monroe's movies strikingly illustrate that American fantasy. In those fairy tales of seduction, men are horny and innocent boys, a little insecure, a little awkward, perhaps even sexually repressed. Instead of assertively seducing women and taking responsibility for their desire, as European men do, they long to lose control and be seduced by a voluptuous and gloriously curvy goddess, pillowy soft and squishy, vulnerable and innocent, yet bursting with female magnetism, who will dominate them and initiate them into the mysteries of sex. Marilyn Monroe's movies might have been born of the fifties' sexual repression. But, from my French perspective, I think they express a deeper—and still valid—truth about the dynamic of the sexes in America.

*all the available light*

## MARILYN AT THE MIKVAH

*Evan Zimroth*

*P*icture this: Marilyn Monroe standing stark naked in a pool of water, her fingers spread out and resting on the surface. Her face is scrubbed free of makeup, her hair newly shampooed, her fingernails clipped and clean. The buxom body is a little plump for our taste, but still ravishingly beautiful; at this moment it is immaculately soaped and rinsed. Every inch and millimeter of her body opens to the flow of the water as she bends her knees. Under she goes, all the way under, her platinum hair rising in tendrils upward as she sinks below the water's surface. Perhaps she holds her breath (as starlets were taught in the fifties) to make it appear as if she is concentrating; perhaps Marilyn blows bubbles. After a moment underwater, she rises to hear an approving voice. "Kosher," it says, or rather, "Ko-sher," with the two syllables slowly drawn out. Marilyn is now a Jew.

Perhaps it didn't happen quite like that.

Monroe was converted to Judaism early in the day on July 1, 1956—22 Tammuz, in the Hebrew calendar—just in time for her afternoon wedding to Arthur Miller. The officiating rabbi was Robert E. Goldburg, a Reform rabbi from New Haven, Connecticut, who had briefly instructed Monroe in the tenets of her new religion. But as a civil liberties activist, Rabbi Goldburg's real tie was to Miller, who had just received a subpoena from the House Un-American Activities Committee. Miller, overwhelmed with anxiety about his upcoming testimony, seems to have been little interested in Monroe's religious convictions. Indeed, in *Timebends,* his autobiography, the playwright devotes several chapters to his HUAC problems, a half-page afterthought to his wedding to Monroe, and not a single sentence to his bride's conversion.

The Monroe-Miller alliance was tense, rushed, and accidentally tragic. The publicity surrounding Miller's HUAC testimony and the upcoming wedding had fast become fatal. Two days earlier, on Friday, June 29, a woman correspondent from *Paris-Match* tailing the couple for a story had been killed in a gruesome car accident when the car skidded and ran into a tree. Monroe and Miller heard the crash and rushed to the scene, where Monroe herself helped to pull the woman's horribly mangled body from the car. In a bizarre decision, Miller decided to marry Monroe at once. So about six hours after the crash, Monroe and Miller were united in a civil ceremony presided over by Judge Seymour Robinowitz at the Westchester County Courthouse in White Plains, New York. They were pronounced husband and wife at 7:21 P.M., an hour before sundown, marking the beginning of Shabbat, the Jewish sabbath. Because no conversions or Jewish weddings can take place on Shabbat, the couple would have to wait until early Sunday for the two Jewish ceremonies.

So it came about that Monroe had a shotgun conversion.

Although Jewish law actually *prohibits* conversion for the sake of marriage, the breakneck pace of events that weekend, however, suggests that the two events were indelibly twinned. Actually, there is no halachic—that is, Jewishly legal—reason to prohibit a conversion from occurring only moments before the wedding, unless the bride might be pregnant. In that case, the *child's* Jewish identity is in question, although not the mother's. This requirement apparently was waived—ignored—in Monroe's case. However, as Jewish law requires, a *beth din,* or legal court of three men, witnessed Monroe's conversion: Arthur Miller's brother Kermit, the rabbi himself, and a third man whose name on Monroe's conversion certificate is illegibly scrawled. The document is also signed by the bridegroom-to-be, a sentimental but religiously unnecessary gesture.

Was *mikvah*—immersion—part of the ritual? Probably not, partly because Reform practice doesn't require it, but also for a more practical reason. After all, Monroe would have had to go from naked immersion in water to bridal dress and wedding coiffure in a matter of hours. And this in a day before high-speed hair-dryers. *Life* magazine, covering the big event (the wedding, of course, not the conversion), photographed a stern Miller and a tremulous Monroe facing the rabbi under the *chuppah,* the wedding canopy. Her every hair is in place. The only difficulty, *Life* reports adoringly, was that the wedding was performed in such haste that the bride had to stain her veil in coffee to match it to her wedding dress. Miller in *Timebends* is more honest: he admits that nothing could dispel the afternoon's tension. After all, in under forty-eight hours the bride witnessed a fatal car crash, converted to Judaism, and was twice married.

From an Orthodox point of view, both the conversion and the marriage are possibly invalid. A Jewish marriage—halachically—must include not only two Jewish participants but also two legal witnesses. Assuming that the same men probably served as witnesses for both conversion and wedding, they could be nullified as legal witnesses by the circumstantial evidence provided by one of the photographs in *Life.* The halachic (or Orthodox) requirement for a marriage witness is that he not only should be unrelated to the bridal couple, but also Sabbath-observant and a follower of *kashrut,* the Jewish dietary laws. This would eliminate Kermit Miller as a legal witness. For the validity of the second witness, the *Life* photograph calls into question the rabbi himself. That photograph captures a moment at the wedding supper when Monroe and Miller have wrapped themselves in a deep embrace as a beaming rabbi looks on. No problem here. The photographer (and Monroe's business partner) Milton Greene has memorialized one of Monroe's happiest moments—the lovely bride encircled by family and friends. The problem is the menu: roast beef, turkey, and lobster. Did the good rabbi eat unkosher meat, not to mention delicious but absolutely forbidden lobster? Quite likely. Although the photograph does not show the rabbi wearing a paper bib and tucking in to a juicy lobster claw, who could say no to such a feast? The little biographical material we have about the rabbi (Monroe biographers do not even agree on the spelling of his name) plus the admittedly circumstantial evidence of Greene's photograph suggest that Rabbi Goldburg was more active as a civil libertarian than as an enforcer of *kashrut*. The photograph radiates sensual pleasure, from the kiss of the newlyweds to the smiles of the relatives to the happy disarray of the table, and everyone belongs to the clean-plate club. Marriage annulled.

But conversion is defined, shall we say, more fluidly.

Ancient Judaism apparently had no fixed rites for conversion. When Ruth the Moabite followed Naomi to Bethlehem, she did not have to immerse herself in a *mikvah* nor was her conversion overseen by a rabbi or *beth din*. Her vow of loyalty was enough: "Thy people shall be my people and thy God my God," as it says on Monroe's conversion certificate. But the Talmud prescribes a variety of rituals for the convert. Conversion then and now requires some instruction in Jewish practice, immersion in a *mikvah* (total immersion for men, sometimes only up-to-the-neck immersion for women), and (for a male) circumcision. But even though the rituals of conversion change, we tend to think as Ruth did—that the convert, like Ruth and like Marilyn after her, takes on the destiny of the Jewish people. Why would Monroe wish to do so?

No one, outside of Monroe herself, seems to have paid much attention to her conversion. Only two writers mention it, briefly and with puzzlement—Norman Rosten, a close friend and member of the wedding party, in his memoir, and Carl Rollyson in a critical analysis of Monroe's work as an actress. Both acknowledge that her conversion cannot be attributed entirely to her marriage, since apparently neither Miller nor his family pressured Monroe to convert.

Miller's values, outlook, and liberal politics, however, are profoundly Jewish. Monroe had read his first novel,

*all the available light*

*Focus* (1945), a study of how anti-Semitism affects identity, well before she met the author. The individual pitted against a repressive, even murderous, culture was a theme that absorbed Miller and deeply attracted Monroe, as well as a respect for the workingman and -woman. The Jew as outsider, refusing to assimilate to the dominant culture, even the Jew as victim, Monroe understood. She could link a Jewish history of pogroms and Holocaust to her own personal history of family neglect, sexual abuse, and far too many sessions on the casting couch. The Jewish paradigm of liberation from slavery must have appealed to her as well, since during the period of her conversion and marriage she had intensified her efforts to finance her own production company in order to become independent of the Hollywood studio system. Twentieth Century-Fox was her Egypt.

But in the end, it was probably the Jewish family that she savored and sought, the *mishpocha:* her husband, his parents and relatives and friends, and, more widely, the Jewish family structure of the Actors Studio with Lee and Paula Strasberg, Monroe's revered teacher and coach, as surrogate parents and heads of the tribe. It was Paula who gave Monroe a Jewish Bible to mark her conversion and Lee, as father, who gave her away at the wedding.

Apparently, the conversion "took"; it lasted. Even after her divorce from Miller, Monroe retained her identity as a Jew, keeping a *mezuzah* for her doorpost and a brass-plated musical menorah for Hanukkah whose base played "Hatikvah," the Israeli national anthem. She seems to have truly considered herself *bat Avraham vSara*, daughter of Abraham and Sarah, who, as legend has it, converted their children and entire household to Judaism. Monroe's conversion document records that "Marilyn Monroe having sought to join the household of Israel and promising to live by its principles and practices was received into the Jewish Faith." Going from *mikvah* to *chuppah* in one tumultuous day, Monroe acquired a new identity and a new sense of historical destiny.[1]

## TWO DAUGHTERS
*Dennis Grunes*

*E*thel Kennedy, the wife, then the widow, of Robert Kennedy, didn't get on well (we now know) with sister-in-law Jacqueline Kennedy. One of Ethel Kennedy's complaints, at the time that her husband was U.S. attorney general in John Kennedy's administration, had to do with her sister-in-law's voice. Ethel found it phony, because Jacqueline sounded so very different in public than she did in private, such as at family gatherings. To be sure, Jacqueline's voice may have been code for her whole personality, as Ethel perceived it—a synecdoche, as it were. But let's take the critic at her (literal) word. I disagree. I don't find the First Lady's adoption in public of a softer, wispier, "breathier" voice the least bit phony; Jacqueline Bouvier's schooling, after all, had surely taught her to suit manner to occasion. But the voice stuck in Ethel's craw. Where did this voice come from? Ethel (in saltier language) wondered—sometimes aloud. But we all know where it came from; it was the cultivated, sexually neutered version of a famous contemporary's voice. It was the voice of Marilyn Monroe.

In retrospect, what irony. John Kennedy had extramarital relations with Monroe. But even this irony returns us to the remarkable hold of Monroe's celebrity. Jacqueline Bouvier Kennedy, one of our nation's loftiest personalities herself, modeled an aspect of her public persona on Marilyn Monroe. What I probably mean is Marilyn Monroe's. For Monroe's voice, instantly recognizable, may also have been part of her public persona, part of her professional act.

As such, it belonged to the public, and Jacqueline Kennedy wasn't alone in appropriating one or more elements of it for herself. Monroe's influence matched the size of her stardom, although this influence could be subtle. It's possible, for example, that Jacqueline Kennedy wasn't aware of whose voice she was copying. Immense celebrity such as Monroe possessed doesn't stay contained in the star herself; it becomes part of the cultural air that people breathe. This, however, was a double-edged sword; it took "Marilyn Monroe" the star away from Marilyn Monroe the woman and sometimes aimed her persona against her. The price of great celebrity is that one becomes the possession, the property, of those who celebrate you. Monroe, no fool, participated in the creation of "Marilyn Monroe"; but Monroe, a fool like the rest of us, didn't foresee the consequences of fashioning herself into a fabulous myth.

Monroe's persona could be described as the dumb blonde with a card or two tucked up her sleeve. This also describes the image that platinum blond Jean Harlow— the "blond bombshell"—projected from the silver screen in the 1930s. But Harlow, although funny like Monroe, was nastier, cruder; she lacked Monroe's sweetness and vulnerability. Each played a number of gold diggers; but one really wanted Monroe to get what she wanted. Harlow seemed a force of ambition; Monroe, a force of nature, and of the lighter side of human nature. This is why comparisons between Marilyn and Madonna also don't quite work. Rather, Madonna is Harlow's true heir.

Monroe's persona was closest of all, perhaps, to that of Marie Wilson, whose career Monroe's own eclipsed. Remember her? In her teens, she was Mary Quite Contrary, with Laurel and Hardy, in *Babes in Toyland* (Gus Meins, Charles Rogers, 1934), and just out of her teens, she was the Sam Spade character's deliciously comic, sweet-natured, sexy secretary in *Satan Met a Lady* (William Dieterle, 1936), a lighthearted version of

Dashiell Hammett's death-hearted *Maltese Falcon*. Wilson's warm, relaxed ditziness blossomed into full-blooded dumb-blondeness in a frenetic satire on Hollywood, *Boy Meets Girl* (Lloyd Bacon, 1938), and Wilson was still turning her delightful act, as Irma Peterson, in *My Friend Irma* (George Marshall, 1949), the film introducing (in a canned rather than live format) Dean Martin and Jerry Lewis. A big hit, this film generated a sequel and a fifties television series, with Wilson repeating her role, now as the principal character.

Wilson was a better, more versatile actress than Monroe, but she wasn't a sex symbol, nor was she capable of projecting such charisma as Monroe does in *Gentlemen Prefer Blondes* (Howard Hawks, 1953) and *Some Like It Hot* (Billy Wilder, 1959). For me, though, Marilyn's richest role fell in between: Elsie Marina, the American showgirl, in Britain at the time of the coronation of George V, in Laurence Olivier's sophisticated and, finally, quite moving film *The Prince and the Showgirl* (1957). Alone and in secret, Elsie breaks into impromptu dance in a palace: a magical moment. But the whole comedy enchants, and not the least so because Monroe's Elsie, out to seduce the visiting Prince Regent of Carpathia, is, however surreptitiously, a match for him and for all the political plots and connivings circling in her midst. Monroe's smartest role, without a trace of her customary victimization, found her irresistibly up to the challenge. However, Monroe herself was disappointed by the experience of doing this film, which is based on Terence Rattigan's play *The Sleeping Prince.* She had hoped that working with Olivier meant being taken seriously as an actress for once; but the role was light, and director Olivier—whose own performance is brilliant—may not have wanted her to search out a character (at least that's how Monroe felt) but simply to bring to her role the airiest, most tender, most intelligent version of herself. In every way, Monroe is beautiful in his film. What a pity there aren't other roles in her œuvre so clear of the taints of victimization and self-pity.

The fact is, it was never Monroe's destiny to be an actress—a Sybil Thorndike, say, who is terrific in the Olivier film playing the Queen Dowager. Perhaps it was the curse of her charisma that Monroe's definition was always going to be "star." Indeed, Monroe announced herself as nothing less than that even in an early small part, as an actress on the make, in *All About Eve* (Joseph L. Mankiewicz, 1950). She constructed this persona of hers on such a large scale, I believe, in order to lose herself in it—and with herself, the unhappy childhood and past we all know about. The proof of her stardom is that she ended up almost everywhere in the American midst (and elsewhere, besides), in the way girls and women, consciously or not, dressed, made up, walked, and—yes—spoke.

ANOTHER PROOF of Monroe's stardom is the attempts of Hollywood studios other than Twentieth Century-Fox, the one that had Monroe under contract, to come up with a Marilyn of their own. However unlikely this may seem to us now, Universal tried converting Shelley Winters, who had been Monroe's roommate, into their Marilyn facsimile; Columbia had better luck with Kim Novak, whose appeal, while falling short of Marilyn's, lunged ahead into territory of palpable sexuality— not the dreamy fantasy of sex that Monroe conjured (in Wilder's *The Seven Year Itch* [1955] she played the figment of a horny guy's imagination), but the real kind that makes men's thighs heat up. However, by far the most remarkable and interesting response came from Paramount. Their Marilyn Monroe was the Not-Marilyn, the Anti-Marilyn: Audrey Hepburn.

Jacqueline Kennedy's shy though easy grace owes as much to Hepburn as her public manner of speaking owes to Monroe; in Kennedy, we see, in fact, the convergence of star influences—for Hepburn's celebrity was every bit as immense, and omnipresent, as Monroe's. Hepburn, too, set styles and gave girls and women someone to emulate. Hepburn also was vulnerable—although more likely to elicit from men protective, paternal feelings than aroused, predatory ones. Hepburn and Monroe were polar opposites—except that, in reality, human qualities exist on a circular, not flat, continuum. We shouldn't be surprised, therefore, to find Hepburn and Monroe, because they are so far apart, in some ways back-to-back.

Monroe's background resembled Joan Crawford's:

poverty, dislocation, loneliness, sexual abuse. (Infamously, Crawford at a formal dinner ridiculed Monroe for not knowing which fork to use for which course—as Monroe herself might have done with someone else twenty years hence, had she lived.) Hepburn's, on the other hand, was a class act from the get-go. Born in Belgium, Edda van Heemstra Hepburn-Ruston was the daughter of an English banker and a Dutch baroness. When Edda was six, her father abandoned the family, just left—"the most traumatic event in my life," Hepburn would later say. Moreover, after her parents' divorce, her father did not avail himself of his visitation rights. By this time, Edda's mother had moved the family—her daughter and two stepsons—to England, but then, disastrously, shifted ground, deciding that things would be safer in her home country, Holland. Hitler invaded, and the Nazi occupation left Edda despondent and rail-thin from malnutrition. One of Edda's stepbrothers was killed by the Nazis. While her father supported Hitler, Edda worked as a sometime courier for the Resistance. She was fifteen by the war's end. She studied ballet and became a model, for which her thinness was advantageous. Eventually, Edda became the Audrey Hepburn we knew: following walk-ons and bit parts in Dutch and British films, the Hollywood star.

Hepburn: Not-Monroe. For instance, Hepburn's elegant skinniness, in reality the repository of the battered childhood she kept mum about, contrasted with Monroe's image of ample flesh. Ironically, this was just an image, an illusion, in one regard—a piece of the sex symbol that Monroe, in concert with others, turned herself into. For, truth be told, Marilyn Monroe's breasts were no more than average in size—no small matter in light of the American male's mammary fixation. But generous padding made Marilyn seem "better" endowed—enormous even. In some quarters, the (apparent) size of her bosom became a target for nervous, derisive sexual humor.

Hepburn's acting was lauded while Monroe's was lambasted. Hepburn collected an Oscar (for William Wyler's *Roman Holiday* [1953]), a Tony the same year (for Jean Anouilh's *Ondine*) and two New York Film Critics' prizes (for *Roman Holiday* and Fred Zinnemann's *Nun's Story* [1959]); but Monroe took cover in the Actors Studio to counter the impression she couldn't act at all. The contrast couldn't be sharper: Hepburn seemed the thoroughly competent, even gifted, professional whose work merited admiration and hosannas, while Monroe seemed the self-deluded, somewhat frantic acting wannabe who, instead of winning prizes, drew bad copy for almost always arriving on the set late.

There was a sense, too, of refinement with Hepburn and vulgarity with Monroe, although filmgoers at the time too often failed to appreciate the delicacy with which Monroe invested her characters once she got past the vicious slut she played in *Niagara* (Henry Hathaway,

*all the available light*

1953). No, I would characterize the difference between
these stars in another way. Whereas Monroe seemed to
exude a sense of the present, even if only as a fantastic
idea or image implanted in some guy's head, Hepburn
seemed somehow always connected to the past. In her
charming, poignant, dreamily romantic comedies (like
the two loveliest, Wilder's *Sabrina* [1954] and *Love in the
Afternoon* [1957]), Hepburn, fragile yet resilient, casts a
haunting backward glance, her elfin smile quietly hiding
(and, really, disclosing) heartbreak. For all the abstraction
implicit in Monroe's sexual iconography, Monroe's
fleshiness as well as her modernity gave her an immedi-
acy, an urgency, that tied her to the here and now. Like
James Dean, Monroe seems to emanate from the tur-
moil repressed beneath the official blandness—middle
America's self-image—of the fifties; but Hepburn, even
before we knew her life story, seemed like a reed in the
wind of stormy recent history—a reminder of what it
had taken for much of the world simply to survive.

It is certainly the case that Hepburn's suggestively
tragic poise—her Europeanness—was as unmistakable as
Monroe's Americanness—her pluckiness amid self-
doubt. However, these two qualities can also be seen as
competing claims on the American spirit, for Ameri-
cans—Monroe included—always had a hankering for
European class, elegance, and prestige. In this context,
Hepburn spoke to the peace, quiet, and emotional foot-
ing we felt we were entitled to for enduring the Second

World War, while Monroe suggested instead the feverish reality of an America that wanted to leave that war behind, that had a new (and terrifying) "cold" war with which to contend, and whose booming economy vis-à-vis conditions in much of the rest of the world made the nation a focal point for the world's future.

Not surprisingly, for all their differences, each of these two female icons resolved into a dominant trait of vulnerability, Hepburn as she evoked a flypaper past, Monroe as she evoked an anxious present that in fact turned out to be a fantastic respite before an all-too-real future of presidential assassination, civil rights upheaval, and war again—but war without the clarity of moral coordinates to locate its necessity in the blunt American consciousness.

On one occasion, a year before the suicide of Monroe and a half-dozen years before the unexpected retirement of Hepburn, the careers of these two actresses obliquely crossed. Hepburn had a huge hit playing Holly Golightly, formerly Lulamae Barnes, in the film version of Truman Capote's *Breakfast at Tiffany's* (Blake Edwards, 1961). Capote, who adored Hepburn and made peace with her performance, never hesitated to say that he had wanted Marilyn to play the call girl.

Indeed, Capote may have written Holly with Monroe in mind. Hepburn, of course, sparkles in the role; but Monroe might have better captured the Lulamae heart behind the Golightly façade.

194     Monroe's unhappy childhood turned her, offscreen, into a perpetual child, a self-centered, perpetually insecure soul who—like Crawford, the "walking wounded"—wore her misery for all to see and never flinched from imposing it on others, including, most willingly, us. Hepburn, the adult, hid her unhappiness and turned outward, in the last phase of her life, from 1988 until her death from cancer in 1993, directing her energies to helping suffering children in Africa and Latin America as special ambassador for the United Nations International Children's Emergency Fund. At the last, then, Hepburn found a way of stilling the ghosts that were always having at her. Not Marilyn, who ended her own life in a wash of self-pity and drugs at thirty-six.

Time has been kind to Monroe. She now elicits the kind of protectiveness that she rarely did during her lifetime—the kind of feelings that more easily went to Audrey Hepburn. In death Marilyn has also become our daughter, and it was as a daughter that she so desperately wanted to make her ultimate claim upon us.

# the sum of the parts: marilyn reconstructed

As you might expect with a movie star of Monroe's proportions, her various parts are worshiped and pored over to the same degree—if not more—than the entire being. The hair, for instance, that began as light brown and metamorphosed into gleaming platinum, or the breasts that at times assume a kind of disembodied, fetishlike importance.

But there are other, more subtle aspects of the Monroe persona that until now have not received their proper due.

In "Mother, Daughter, Siren, Lover," novelist Lisa Shea turns her attention to Monroe's oft-neglected singing voice. Has anyone given serious consideration to the lyrics of Monroe's songs, or to the inimitable way she sang them? Like a wise and patient friend, Shea listens deeply and attentively to Monroe's voice and writes about what she hears.

Melissa Pierson's essay "The Hunted" attempts to dissect and understand Marilyn's various expressions, gestures, and body language as those of something wild and not quite human. Pierson, whose most recent nonfiction book is *Dark Horses and Black Beauties,* has what might be perhaps called an uncommon affinity for—and perhaps even with—animals. So, she persuasively argues, did Monroe.

"Reliquary," the final essay in this volume, brings the Monroe story up to date by describing the recent postmortem of Monroe's earthly possessions: the auction at Christie's at which the faithful bid for the remaining pieces of her life that they might own and cherish in her stead.

# MOTHER, DAUGHTER, SIREN, LOVER: MARILYN IN SONG
*Lisa Shea*

The first movie I saw Marilyn Monroe in was *Some Like It Hot*. Her fleshy, brazenly grown-up (I was nine) yet somehow innocent appearance as she wiggled, giggled, and sang her way through Billy Wilder's wacky, gender-bending comedy produced in me a tumult of feelings—fascination, envy, embarrassment, fear. The dress she wore—virtually see-through except for the sequins—on her steamy date scene with Tony Curtis aboard his borrowed yacht, still floats in my mind as an icon of shimmering, nonpareil womanhood.

Years later, I was shocked to learn that Monroe had hated the film, claiming it made her look like "a funny fat pig."

While her form was formidable, what always has intrigued me most about Monroe is her voice. Over the years, watching (and rewatching) films like *Some Like It Hot* and *Gentlemen Prefer Blondes, Niagara, The Seven Year Itch,* and *How to Marry a Millionaire,* I've been delighted and perplexed by the girlish, even babyish, yet sultry and seductive (not to mention comedic) qualities her voice embodies and which, like everything else about her, contains such wild contradictions. In songs like "I Want to Be Loved by You," "Some Like It Hot," and "We're Having a Heat Wave," all collected on *The Very Best of Marilyn Monroe* CD from Stardust Records, her range veers from cotton-candy sweet to stiletto high-heel sexy, while her signature vocal purr is as kittenish as it is childlike.

Not blessed with a real singer's voice, Monroe instead mined brilliantly what she did possess—mood, perceptiveness, emotion. Listen to the vulnerable quiver that shadows her otherwise rowdy vocal exuberance in "Diamonds Are a Girl's Best Friend"; the insouciant syllabics that surface in "My Heart Belongs to Daddy" when she semi–scat–sings "da da da da da da"; the whispering wistfulness permeating the ballad "River of No Return"; the gently honky-tonk, game phrasing she pulls off in "I'm Gonna File My Claim," where she teases "Looking for nuggets?"

But my favorite song by Monroe on this compilation is "Down in the Meadow." Surprisingly, it's a lullaby. I have fallen asleep listening to this sweet, chaste song, feeling so safe and comforted that I forget it is sung by a woman whose life was dangerously fraught virtually from the moment she was born. That Monroe could sing in a voice so at odds with the famously exaggerated, clichéd postures and poses that lent her cascading shape an impression of eroticized flesh barely being contained, that she possessed a voice that could be clear and un-adorned, even maternal, is a marvel.

I love listening to "Meadow" not only at night but when I'm feeling lost or upset or sad, when I am in need of a motherly fix, if only for the two minutes and twenty-five seconds the song lasts, with Monroe singing, "Down in the meadow under the snow, April is teaching green things to grow. . . . Down in the meadow, corn stalks are high, pumpkins are ripe and ready for pie. . . ." Nothing bad happens in the song; all is seasonal, natural, peaceful. Sometimes, if I am still awake near the song's end, I drift off to the lullaby's last stanza, which captures Monroe's voice at its most angelic as she softly coos, "Down in the meadow, snow softly gleams, earth goes to sleep and smiles in her dreams."

The extreme of this exercise in the vocal sublime is, of course, the sloppy, surreal "Happy Birthday" riff she sang to President Kennedy in 1962 after being intro-duced by Kennedy in-law and celebrity Peter Lawford. "Mr. President," he slickly intones (as if they needed an introduction!), "Marilyn Monroe." After a conspicuously long pause, Monroe begins her alcohol-and-pill-fueled, half-sung, half-spoken salute, sounding more like a supremely troubled soul than an icon of temptation. Amid the sporadic applause and nervous laughter that erupts from the audience during the recording, Monroe finally just sounds painfully, irretrievably alone. Three months later, in August of that year, she was found naked in bed, phone in hand, dead of a drug overdose. She was thirty-six.

WHEN I GO back to my early impressions of Marilyn Monroe, I see her luminous platinum hair and pouty red-polished lips, her face either radiant with joy and ready to celebrate, or stung with hurt and ready to crumple, and her impossibly curvy body sashaying around in a riotous slew of sex goddess getups. When I listen to her sing, I can move beyond those fixed visual markers and concentrate on the emotional nuance of her voice, the mix of naïveté, naughtiness, and sheer chutz-pah she so seamlessly projected.

The three notes Monroe hums at the beginning of the Western-style ballad "River of No Return," from the 1954 Otto Preminger film of that title, are little mas-terpieces of mood. So, too, is the whole of "She Acts Like a Woman Should," also from the Preminger movie, the hopelessly outdated lyrics of which do nothing to dampen the song's dreamy appeal. Monroe's voice literally seems to mature from adolescent to adult during the course of "When I Fall in Love" despite the mawkish strings and chorus accompaniment. And she sounds so knowledgeable-in-love in "A Fine Romance" and so helpless-in-love in "When Love Goes Wrong" when she and Jane Russell, sharing lyrics, lament, "It's like we said, You're better off dead/When love has lost its glow/So take this down in black and white/When love goes wrong nothing goes right."

Those words take on an eerie resonance when you lift them out of the Monroe songbook and apply them to her brief, tempestuous life. The gift she had of conjuring such raw and ready emotion in song seemed only to work against her in reality. Addictions, miscarriages, failed marriages, ruinous affairs, and multiple suicide attempts marked her adult life as surely as her triumphs, and with more lasting effect.

But the magic of listening to Monroe is that no matter what she's singing about, her voice wraps you up in diamonds and fur; she puts out, in the best sense of the term, as mother, daughter, siren, lover. Listening, you feel special, the way she always wanted to feel, and so rarely, authentically did. As she confides in "Do It Again," chillingly miming what seems to have been the central drama of her life, "Oh, no one is near, I may cry Oh, oh, oh, but no one will hear." The sentiment may be brutally dark, but the voice is pure pink champagne.

*all the available light*

## THE HUNTED
*Melissa Holbrook Pierson*

The most trite and tattered bit of them all is
that she was some sort of mirror in which we
could see ourselves reflected; that she became whatever
we wished her to be. More likely, that is what she became when we decided not to see. Because to look at
her is to look at a truth so long and hard and obvious it
might as well be the sidewalk under our feet.

Here are a few small details. The eyebrows, perma-
nently frozen in the cocked stretch of a tern's two wings
in flight. The way she sometimes talks, breathily stumbling over words as if the whole notion of speech is as

foreign as a monkey's learning to type. The preening. Often, a sudden look that could only be called a deer caught in headlights: damaged, frantic to flee. That one time in the movie when she fights like a wild animal to escape the man who has suddenly thrown his weight on top of her. The analysis of her behavior that runs to dozens of volumes and counting, a challenge to the number of studies we produce on any alien species we wish to understand. That which she recalls, to the boors at least: a kitten, a chick. So she is hunted, and people long to have her in their sights.

How could we have missed it? (There were all those observations: from others—"She struck me as kind of fey, as not being altogether in this world"; "If she saw a dead dog in the road, she'd cry"—and from herself—"I can understand the salmon. I've felt like them.") The books about her keep appearing in our insatiable need to comprehend her. And indeed, as soon as you write one thing, another needs to be written on top of it. Her qualities wouldn't stay still: ditzy, certainly, but wise and self-knowing, too; afraid but ambitious, like she had the taste of blood in her mouth; fragile and wounded, yet bent on self-destruction; kind, empathic, gentle, but mean and negligent at times.

IN ELEMENTARY-SCHOOL science we learned about predator and prey, about how the two were never one. Then we grew up and figured out that this was a lie.

AS A DISCARDED child, she first learned that "devotion" was a word that had a meaning by tutoring under the brown eyes of a small dog named Tippy. They stuck to her at all times. It must have amazed her, just as those presents that materialize under a cut evergreen one sudden day, how quickly this thing could grow, how reciprocal it was. He went with her to school, waited in the yard, went home with her at day's end. Wherever she was to be found, so was he.

Then, in the lostness of the night, he was gone, shot, probably, by a neighbor. This is the place in the story where, it is indicated, we all should cry. The remainder of it will detail her resultant wounded empathy with all living creatures.

Yes, well, not so fast. As a young wife, on the cusp of discovery by an adoring public of men, there is another tale of canine devotion, this one, too, ending in death, although the bullet (as it were) was fired by her. Muggsie, the faithful collie, soon abandoned to a back porch at her in-laws' while she went on calls to seduce the lens, languished as only a pack animal can languish. Without her, day in and day out alone, he simply could not live.

She may well have caused her playwright husband to write a story titled "Please Don't Kill Anything," inspired by her desperate attempts once to rescue fishermen's rejected catch by throwing them back into the sea, but that night she no doubt ate the finned beings who had passed the humans' test of worthiness. She may well have wept small brooks of tears for the warm-blooded targets of her first husband's rifle (one time a deer, still alive, a hunter's true sin and shame, that she tried to save), but not so for the hundreds of flayed ermines, minks, and beavers whose skins embraced her own. Out of sight, out of mind. This is the credo by which she lived. By which we all live, animals whose infernal complexity is so thoroughgoing it alone makes us human.

THE QUESTION ISN'T really one of empathy, although it plays a role. It isn't really who or what she *allied* with, it is what she *was*.

The Mason-Dixon line in our civil war with the rest of creation has bizarrely been drawn along language—because we confuse speech with language. And because we simply do not recognize the form of language that other species use. (As if, anyway, talking has something to do with a right to live.) But she does. It is her primary mode of communication, used precisely and to brilliant effect: body language. Not just the pendulum of hips, but the eyes, their direction and somnolence, the head, its cock and turn, the step, rising up on toes or crouched, even at a run.

It would be easiest to forget that we began as animals

(we can hum a sunny tune as we kill, grind our brethren into food, torture, hunt, kill), that we still are animals. We push away this truth as if our lives depended on it, although only the animals' really do. Then there she is, reminding us. Strangely, it is a comfort. We can be what we are again.

See, we *are* complex.

THE PLACE TO see it all expressed is the last movie, *The Misfits,* which was her swan song. Written for her, about her, it is full of contradictions and proclamations and suggestions. (Its plot, such as it is, may have been influenced by A. J. Liebling's 1954 *New Yorker* piece about similar men who hunt the wild horses of the West so they might nourish the pets of America: in it, the author's wife also protests the cruelty of "The Mustang Buzzers," even encouraging a stallion to escape, while it is pointed out that at home she feeds her cat on identical meat.)

When our misfit sees an injustice, she does not give it a jury trial. She reacts (like an animal) and expresses her outrage not in words but with her entire being (like an animal). This is not to say that the logic is not impeccable; it is (like an animal's). Thus, when she notices the bucking strap cinched tight around the rodeo bronc's tender groin:

"It's not fair!"

"They wouldn't have a rodeo otherwise," goes the whiny protest.

"They shouldn't have the rodeo." With that rejoinder, impeccable truth, she moves to leave.

In the movie, she befriends a dog and becomes distraught at the possibility that a rabbit will be shot. But it is the wild horses that unhinge her, and she fights as savagely as they do against their ropes. When she retreats to a distant small point in the center of the frame, she becomes larger. When she screams, she is taken over, is something else. (As in that earlier film, *Bus Stop*, which some consider the first to test her real skills, where she comes unglued to yell, in beautiful fury and purely reactive redundancy: "I hate you and I despise you!")

In that moment where she stands with the horses, complex creatures too, the truth is long and hard and finally obvious. Like us, she shares their fate, for she is like them. An animal, fierce and gorgeous and marked for death.

## RELIQUARY
*Yona Zeldis McDonough*

All brass, glass, and serenely ascending escalators, Christie's streamlined new gallery space at 20 Rockefeller Plaza in Manhattan seems to owe its architectural inspiration to a contemporary commercial emporium rather than to any sacred space. Yet for the period of time leading up to what may have been the most significant celebrity auction of the last millennium, Christie's did indeed become a kind of hallowed ground. It was then that the possessions of Marilyn Monroe were displayed for the rapt crowds who came—curious, avid, supplicating—to view and ultimately buy them.

The fifteen hundred items—clothing, furniture, decorative items, books, and papers—on exhibit at Christie's had been bequeathed by Monroe to her mentor, Lee Strasberg. When Strasberg died in 1982, they became the property of his second wife, Anna. Mrs. Strasberg's motive in selling them, seventeen years later, remains unclear. But to the Monroe worshipers who thronged through the building to inhale their long-dormant perfume, their aromatic dust, motive was immaterial. All the faithful cared about was coming face-to-face with the relics—worn, precious, holy—that affirmed the woeful humanity of their patron saint, Marilyn herself.

What did she leave behind, this paragon of Tinseltown, this bottle blonde with the luminous skin and even more luminous smile? What was it that we were searching for as we gazed upon the remnants of her earthly life? And what did we find?

Christie's treated Monroe's possessions with the scholarly precision usually reserved for Old Master paintings or Ming vases. The thick, clothbound exhibition catalog alone cost nearly $100. Inside it were dozens of full-color photographs and precise descriptions itemizing her personal effects. The effect of this exposure was both intimate and morbid. It was as if the public were catapulted back to a time shortly after Monroe's death when friends and relatives sifted through the possessions of the deceased, sorting, arranging, trying to make sense of a life as they held its external trappings in their hands. That the world should, metaphorically speaking, be invited into

Marilyn Monroe's closet to help dispose of her things seems, in a way, quite fitting for the woman who famously once commented that she belonged to her public since she had never really belonged to anyone else.

So what was there to see, to inspect, to wonder about, either leafing through the pages of the hefty catalog or walking through the galleries at 20 Rockefeller Plaza? For one thing, there was a black five-tiered makeup case, whose tidy, rectangular compartments resembled one of the intricate and mystery-filled constructions by the artist Joseph Cornell. The case was loaded with the tools of Marilyn's trade: lipsticks, cream eye shadows in gold-toned tubes with elegiac names like Pearly Blue and Autumn Smoke. But these were hardly the pristine, fresh-from-the-department-store packages that we might recognize from the world of advertising. Instead, it was clear that everything had been opened, used, and even (slightly) abused. How humble seemed the round tablet of rouge with its soiled sponge, the flattened tube of Helena Rubinstein mascara, the feathery false eyelashes asleep in their small, square box. Even the insides of the drawers were smeared with streaks of coral lipstick or rouge.

These artifacts silently attest to the unmistakable humanity of their owner. But they also reminded us of the artifice—another name for magic—that she used to invent herself. For Marilyn Monroe was an invention, one that took curlers and bobby pins, brushes and pencils, to construct. Her cosmetics then hold a dual meaning: they underscore her mortality while at the same time they were the very means by which she would ultimately escape it.

The clothing she left behind—which represents a large part of her estate—was remarkable for a number of reasons. Christie's neatly divides it into two distinct categories, day wear and evening attire. A useful split, which is somehow suggestive of so many other splits she embodied: goddess and mortal, woman and child, virgin and whore; she ran the symbolic gamut, Marilyn did.

The day wear is chic, classy, and stylish, the wardrobe of a woman who knew her own taste and how to highlight her own considerable attributes. Blouses of ivory silk or satin, capri pants in black, copper, orange, and gray. An elegant ivory cotton coat from Bergdorf Goodman. Simple silk jersey shells and Pucci dresses in delicious, sherbert-inspired colors: raspberry, melon, cherry, mango, and lemon. Accessories like the straw bag, sandals, sun hats, and tortoiseshell headbands which, cleanly laid out in the catalog photograph, resemble nothing so much as accoutrements for a vintage, albeit life-size, Barbie doll.

The evening wear is, by its nature, more sumptuous. Yet it is also curiously more restricted than the daytime clothing. It's as if Monroe were mentally paring down the options to the few that suited her best. Black and white predominate: she owned dozens of black dresses, both short and long, in silk jersey, crepe, velvet, and lace. There is a sleek, ivory-satin evening coat with mother of pearl buttons, a white ivory silk dress from Galanos as well as another white dress with plaited shoestring straps. There are extravagant ostrich boas in white and black, immaculate beige kid evening gloves, evening stoles in champagne silk satin or sable, mink, and fox.

Both the day and evening wear sections of the catalog feature many pairs of her shoes, like the stiletto-heeled pumps from Ferragamo that she favored, and purchased in a variety of materials and colors: scarlet satin encrusted with matching rhinestones, black satin decorated with a cluster of circular rhinestones. Even more than the clothes, the shoes show clear evidence of having been worn: the toes are pushed out; the insides are slightly discolored with perspiration. The high-heeled gold-leather ankle-strap sandals that she wore to entertain the American troops in Korea in 1954 are perhaps the most poignant example: the fragile gold leather peels away from one heel, the insoles are visibly stained and bear, quite literally, the imprint of her feet.

The furniture and decorative objects she left behind are, for the most part, undistinguished. The one notable exception is the lacquered white baby grand piano. But here it is sentiment that plays a large role in its distinction. The piano had belonged to Marilyn's mother Gladys. After Gladys was institutionalized, the piano was sold. It took Marilyn years of searching to find it and buy it back. Even within her lifetime, the piano was an important symbol, one that she went to great lengths to retrieve, as if her damaged girlhood might be retrieved and restored along with it.

Finally, though, Marilyn's possessions seem hardly more than ordinary, especially given her fame and her reputation. No precious antiques to sit on or gaze at, no fabulous works of art to compel and inspire. There were books, though, lots of them. Beckett, Freud, Flaubert, Hemingway, and Steinbeck are all represented in her library, along with many other prominent writers. Did she read them? Hard to know. That she bought them, though, wanted to have them near her, signals something. An aspiration, perhaps, of a self that she didn't have the opportunity—or the time—to realize.

But there is more, too. Marilyn's driver's license, her battered suitcase with its dog-eared travel tags still attached, her clocks and her teacups, her blankets and potato press, her flour sifter and jauntily striped Pelican cooler—all these most extraordinary, ordinary things that broke our hearts because, after all, they are the small, tangible pieces of her own. Here was the mortal woman inside or beneath the image she both invented and projected; here were the small and precious things that sustained her. If we had them, we reasoned, why then, we had her.

Or so it must have seemed to the eager buyers, the people who came to look, but more important, to acquire and possess the last remaining parts of her. The bidding was fast and furious that night at Christie's, and the prices of many items far exceeded their estimated value. Three pairs of blue denim jeans Marilyn wore while filming *River of No Return* sold for $37,000, significantly more than the $20,000 to $30,000 estimated in the catalog. The scarlet satin Ferragamo shoes, estimated at $4,000 to $6,000, actually fetched $42,000. The famous dress—a full-length evening sheath of "flesh-colored soufflé gauze encrusted with graduated rhinestones embroidered in a rosette motif" in which she crooned "Happy Birthday" to America's most charismatic president was sold for over $1 million. (At the gallery, it was spotlighted in a dramatically darkened alcove all its own; in the catalog, it is given a three-page spread—like a triptych—that shows it from different angles.)

History is replete with the finely wrought reliquaries patiently crafted to contain its holy objects: the drops of saints' blood or bone, bits of cloth, scraps of shredded fabric. Relics, notes art historian Kenneth Silver, have meaning only for true believers. For everyone else, they are simply refuse: useless junk, hardly worth the bother. But the people who attended the preview, made bids at the auction, carted home their precious booty, were among the most ardently faithful. Marilyn Monroe was, perhaps, our last and most beloved secular saint, her impossibly buoyant flesh sacrificed to and for her adoring audience, her untimely death a tragic but also necessary precondition of her exalted state. That's what the bidders, buyers, and even just those of us who simply looked understood as we came in droves to Christie's to claim her, finally and irrevocably, as one of our own.

# *chronology*

JUNE 1, 1926  Marilyn Monroe is born in Los Angeles General Hospital, third child of Gladys Pearl Baker, née Monroe. The name on the birth certificate is Norma Jeane (Marilyn later drops the *e* in Jeane). Her father remains unknown. Although the name Mortensen also appears on the birth certificate (Gladys had been married to a man of this name two years earlier), Marilyn denies that he was in fact her father.

JANUARY 1935  Norma Jeane's mother is diagnosed as a paranoid schizophrenic and later committed to Norwalk State Asylum. Gladys's best friend, Grace McKee, is declared Norma Jeane's guardian. Because McKee is a single woman, she takes Norma Jeane to the Los Angeles Orphans Home Society.

1937  Grace McKee marries "Doc" Goddard and takes Norma Jeane in again. Over the next several years, Norma Jeane is shuttled back and forth between foster homes and the orphanage.

JUNE 19, 1942  Norma Jeane Baker marries Jim Dougherty, a match arranged by Grace McKee when she and her husband decided to move east. Norma Jeane is just sixteen years old.

JUNE 26, 1945  An army photographer named Dave Conover takes pictures of Norma Jeane, who is employed at the Radio Plane Corporation. The pictures appear in *Yank,* an army magazine, and Norma Jeane's career as a model is launched.

JULY 17, 1946  Norma Jeane has her first audition with Ben Lyon at Twentieth Century-Fox. In August of the same year, she is given her first studio contract with Fox and changes her name to Marilyn Monroe.

SEPTEMBER 13, 1946  Marilyn divorces James Dougherty.

EARLY 1947  Marilyn is given a bit part in *Scudda Hoo! Scudda Hay!* The film is shown in 1948, after the release of her second film, *Dangerous Years.*

AUGUST 25, 1947  Marilyn's contract with Fox is not renewed.

1948  Marilyn appears in *Ladies of the Chorus,* playing the part of a burlesque queen, Peggy Martin.

EARLY 1949  Groucho Marx helps Marilyn land a small part in *Love Happy.*

MAY 27, 1949  Marilyn poses for Tom Kelley; the nude photographs he takes are used in a calendar.

AUGUST 15, 1949  Filming begins for *A Ticket to Tomahawk,* a Western, in which Marilyn plays the role of Clara, a chorus girl.

JANUARY 5, 1950  Shooting begins for *The Fireball,* in which Marilyn is cast as Polly, a roller-skating groupie.

1950  Marilyn appears in *Right Cross,* with June Allyson, Dick Powell, and Lionel Barrymore. She plays the part of Powell's girlfriend.

JUNE 1950  *The Asphalt Jungle* premieres. Marilyn plays Angela Phinlay, the young mistress of a wealthy and corrupt politician. Later that year, Marilyn is given a seven-year contract with Twentieth Century-Fox. She also has a memorable role as a starlet in the 1950 *All About Eve,* starring Bette Davis, Celeste Holm, and Anne Baxter.

1951  Marilyn plays the role of Miss Martin, a secretary in *Hometown Story.*

1951  Marilyn again appears as a secretary in *As Young as You Feel.*

APRIL 18, 1951  Shooting begins for *Love Nest,* in which Marilyn plays Roberta Stevens, an ex-WAC.

1952  Marilyn plays a gold digger in *Let's Make It Legal,* which starred Claudette Colbert, Macdonald Carey, and Zachary Scott.

1952  Marilyn has a part as Peggy, a fish cannery worker, in the drama *Clash by Night.*

1952  Marilyn is a beauty queen in *We're Not Married,* which also stars Zsa Zsa Gabor.

1952  Acting against type, Marilyn plays a deranged baby-sitter in *Don't Bother to Knock,* which also stars Richard Widmark and Anne Bancroft.

1952  Once again, Marilyn is the dumb blonde in Howard Hawks's *Monkey Business.*

1952  Marilyn lands the role of a streetwalker in *O. Henry's Full House.*

MARCH 13, 1952  The story of the nude calendar photographs appears; Marilyn says she posed because she badly needed the money. The "scandal" caused by her nudity quickly becomes a publicity success, when reporters and fans are touched and charmed by the frank admission of her poverty.

LATE 1952  Filming of *Gentlemen Prefer Blondes* begins. Marilyn is given the coveted role of Lorelei Lee. The movie is a great success in 1953, as is Marilyn's other film of that year, *Niagara,* in which she plays an unfaithful wife.

JUNE 26, 1953  Along with Jane Russell, her costar in *Gentlemen Prefer Blondes,* Marilyn kneels on the sidewalk in front of Grauman's Chinese Theater (Hollywood's famous movie palace) to leave her hand and footprints in the wet cement.

SEPTEMBER 13, 1953  Marilyn makes her first TV appearance on *The Jack Benny Show.*

NOVEMBER 4, 1953  Premier of *How to Marry a Millionaire,* in which Marilyn and her two friends (played by Lauren Bacall and Betty Grable) rent a posh apartment in the hopes of snaring a trio of rich husbands. The film is highly successful and enhances Marilyn's reputation as a star.

DECEMBER 15, 1953  Shooting begins for *The Girl in the Pink Tights.* Although Marilyn is the main box-office attraction, she is paid only $1,500 a week, considerably less than her costar, Frank Sinatra, who receives $5,000. She protests by refusing to show up and is suspended by Fox.

JANUARY 14, 1954  Marilyn marries Joe DiMaggio, a former baseball star. Fox drops the disciplinary measures resulting from her breach of contract.

AUGUST 10, 1954  Filming begins for *The Seven Year Itch*. Directed by Billy Wilder, it tells the story of a married man (played by Tom Ewell) who is obsessed with his lovely neighbor, played by Marilyn.

OCTOBER 27, 1954  Marilyn files for divorce from DiMaggio. The divorce is finalized the following year.

1954  Marilyn, as a saloon singer, stars with Robert Mitchum in Otto Preminger's *River of No Return*.

1954  Acting alongside such legends as Ethel Merman, Donald O'Connor, Dan Dailey, and Mitzi Gaynor, Marilyn plays the part of Vicky, a nightclub singer, in Walter Lang's *There's No Business Like Show Business*.

1954–1955  Marilyn exiles herself from Hollywood and forms Marilyn Monroe Productions with photographer Milton Greene. She seeks psychiatric help for her many emotional problems.

SPRING 1955  Marilyn begins working with famous acting and drama coach Lee Strasberg.

FEBRUARY 1956  Marilyn returns to Hollywood.

MAY 1956  Shooting begins for *Bus Stop,* directed by Joshua Logan. When the shooting is finished, she returns to New York.

MAY 14, 1956  The cover story in *Time* magazine is about Marilyn Monroe.

JUNE 29, 1956  Marilyn marries playwright Arthur Miller, whom she had met some years earlier.

JULY 14, 1956  The bride and bridegroom arrive in London, where they announce Marilyn's newest project, *The Prince and the Showgirl,* in which she will costar with Sir Laurence Olivier. During the stressful shooting of the film, her New York psychiatrist is flown to England so she can continue her treatment.

SPRING 1957. The partnership with Milton Greene falls apart.

AUGUST 1, 1957  Marilyn has a miscarriage, which results in a deep depression and her first suicide attempt.

AUGUST 4, 1958  Shooting commences for *Some Like It Hot,* a comedy directed by Billy Wilder. Marilyn plays Sugar Kane, a singer in an all-girl band. Although she caused huge problems on the set and had many complaints—she didn't get along with costar Tony Curtis, she was disappointed by her other costar, Jack Lemmon (who had been brought in to replace Frank Sinatra), and the fact the film was shot in black-and-white—*Some Like It Hot* went on to become the most successful comedy ever on-screen.

SEPTEMBER 19, 1958  Marilyn is admitted to Cedars of Lebanon Hospital for "nervous exhaustion."

EARLY 1960  Marilyn begins filming *Let's Make Love,* directed by George Cukor and also starring Yves Montand.

MARCH 8, 1960  Marilyn receives the Golden Globe Award as Best Actress in a Comedy for her role in *Some Like It Hot.*

JULY 18, 1960  Filming of *The Misfits* begins in Nevada. Arthur Miller wrote the script for Marilyn and the film is directed by John Huston. Marilyn shares the spotlight with her childhood idol, Clark Gable, and Montgomery Clift. In August, she suffers a nervous breakdown and is flown to a hospital in Los Angeles. She returns to location in September and the shooting is completed in November.

JANUARY 20, 1961  Divorce from Arthur Miller is granted.

FEBRUARY 7, 1961  Admitted to the Payne Whitney Psychiatric Clinic of New York Hospital. Although she leaves in

*all the available light*

March, she is hospitalized again twice more that year and is not able to work.

NOVEMBER 19, 1961  Meets President John F. Kennedy at Peter Lawford's beach house in Santa Monica.

FEBRUARY 1962  Marilyn moves to Brentwood, California. Her home is not far from Peter Lawford's villa, and she continues to meet John and young Robert Kennedy there.

MARCH 1962  Receives Golden Globe Award as World's Film Favorite.

APRIL 23, 1962  Filming for *Something's Got to Give* begins. Marilyn is in very poor physical and emotional condition.

MAY 19, 1962  At John F. Kennedy's birthday celebration at Madison Square Garden, Marilyn sings "Happy Birthday" and "Thanks for the Memory" to fifteen thousand cheering Democrats.

JUNE 8, 1962  Owing to Marilyn's frequent inability to arrive on the set, or to function when she does appear, filming of *Something's Got to Give* is halted and the studio sues her for half a million dollars. Ultimately, they withdraw their charges and plans are made to finish the film by the end of the year.

JUNE 23, 1962  Photo shoot with Bert Stern, commissioned by *Vogue* magazine.

AUGUST 4, 1962  Marilyn's last day. U.S. Attorney General Robert Kennedy visits her, and a doctor who accompanies him gives her a tranquilizer to calm her.

AUGUST 5, 1962  Marilyn Monroe's dead body is found in her Brentwood home. She held a telephone in one hand; an empty bottle of sleeping pills was nearby.

AUGUST 8, 1962  Marilyn Monroe is laid to rest in a crypt in Westwood Memorial Park Chapel.

# notes

## THE "LOVE GODDESS" WHO NEVER FOUND ANY LOVE

1. Monroe's mother, Gladys Pearl Monroe Baker, had been married to Edward Mortensen two years before Monroe's birth, and his name is given on the birth certificate.

## LOOKING GOOD

1. Several sources, most notably Barbara Leaming's *Marilyn Monroe* (Crown, 1998), document Monroe's sexual problems, including the difficulty she had achieving orgasm.

## WE WOULD HAVE HAD TO INVENT HER

1. Joe E. Brown played the millionaire besotted with Jack Lemmon's female alter ego, Daphne.

## FACE VALUE

1. Friedan, *The Feminine Mystique* (New York: Dell, 1963), p. 53.

2. Haskell, *From Reverence to Rape: The Treatment of Women in the Movies,* 2nd. ed. (Chicago & London: University of Chicago Press, 1987; first published by Holt, Rinehart & Winston, New York, 1974), p. 254.

3. See Butler's *Gender Trouble: Feminism and the Subversion of Identity* (New York & London: Routledge, 1990), and *Bodies That Matter: On the Discursive Limits of Sex* (New York & London: Routledge, 1993).

4. Turim, "Gentlemen Consume Blondes," in Bill Nichols, ed., *Movies and Methods,* vol. 2 (Berkeley, Calif.: University of California Press, 1985), p. 373.

5. Postwar America, observes Lynn Spigel, was "a world

where the gendered balance of social and economic power were undergoing change." See Spigel, "The Domestic Economy of Television Viewing in Postwar America," in *Critical Studies in Mass Communication* 6 (1989), p. 352. Also see Stephanie Coontz, *The Way We Never Were: American Families and the Nostalgia Trap* (New York: Basic Books, 1992); Peter Filene, *Him/Her/Self: Sex Roles in Modern America* (Baltimore: Johns Hopkins Press, 1986); Elaine Tyler May, *Homeward Bound: American Families in the Cold War Era* (New York: Basic Books, 1988). For a detailed account of the sorts of cultural materials used to construct fifties femininity, see Douglas T. Miller and Marion Nowak, *The Fifties: The Way We Really Were* (Garden City, N.Y.: Doubleday, 1977).

6. Turim, "Gentlemen Consume Blondes," p. 376.

7. Ibid.

8. Turim, "Designing Women: The Emergence of the New Sweetheart Line," in *Fabrications: Costume and the Female Body* (New York & London: Routledge, 1990, Jane Gaines and Charlotte Herzog, eds.), p. 227.

9. Art historian Barbara A. Schreier's helpful phrase, from her *Mystique and Identity: Women's Fashions of the 1950s* (Norfolk, Va.: Chrysler Museum, 1984).

10. In vol. 186.2, as quoted by Schreier of *Variety, Mystique and Identity*, p. 6.

11. See 1952 and 1953 issues of *Variety* (usually front or second page) for multiple examples of the homophobic and misogynist treatment of Jorgensen (e.g., *Variety,* 12/24/52 [189.3], p. 1; 8/53 [192.7], p. 2; 11/53, [192.10], p. 2). Ed Wood's *Glen or Glenda: "I Changed My Sex"* (billed as "the most shocking film of 1953") and its media reception provide further evidence of the paranoia and hysteria unleashed by the possibility that femininity is performance into which one needn't necessarily have been born.

12. That strategy paid off, as a comparison of the 1952 and 1953 December issues of *Variety Weekly* indicates: on 12/17/52, *Variety* (189.2) reports that top executives at Twentieth Century-

Fox were asked to take a voluntary but drastic pay cut for 1953. The scheme called for a flat 50 percent reduction in all salaries over $500 a week, with the loss restorable at the end of the year if profits warranted (p. 3). A year later, on 12/16/53, *Variety* (193.2) reports that the per-share earnings of Twentieth Century-Fox for 1953 were a record high due to the strong CinemaScope box office in the fourth quarter.

13. I do not wish to imply that such an approach to Monroe (or to Hollywood cinema) will be rewarding in all cases or for all viewers.

### THE PRINCE AND THE SHOWGIRL

1. This comment refers to Olivier's first wife, actress Jill Esmond, as well as his second wife, Vivien Leigh. His extramarital dalliances had been common knowledge by the time this autobiography was published.

### MARILYN AT THE *MIKVAH*

1. Although there is almost no biographical information on Monroe's conversion, for general biographical information, I used two books primarily: Barbara Leaming, *Marilyn Monroe* (New York: Three Rivers Press, 1998); and Carl Rollyson, *Marilyn Monroe: A Life of the Actress* (New York: Da Capo Press, 1993). For patterns of conversion, I relied on Shaye J. D. Cohen, *The Beginnings of Jewishness: Boundaries, Varieties, Uncertainties* (Berkeley: University of California Press, 1999), as well as conversations with various rabbis.

The rabbi who performed both the conversion and the wedding, Rabbi Robert E. Goldburg, had a long and prosperous tenure (1948–1982) at Congregation Mishkan Israel in New Haven, Conn. During his rabbinate, the synagogue hosted almost every left-liberal activist of note, including Daniel Ellsberg, William Sloane Coffin, Carey McWilliams, Martin Luther King, Jr.—and Arthur Miller. Rabbi Goldburg died on July 11, 1995.

*all the available light*

# *about the contributors*

RICHARD B. WOODWARD has written about photography for numerous publications, including *The New York Times Magazine, Vanity Fair, Aperture, Vogue,* and the *Village Voice.* He has contributed catalog essays on contemporary photographers as diverse as Irving Penn and David Levinthal and is the author of seven monographs in the Smithsonian Institution Press "Photographers at Work" series. A book editor for ten years, he now works as editor-at-large for *Double Take* magazine and lives in New York City.

JOYCE CAROL OATES has written some of the most enduring and controversial fiction of our time, including *Blonde, Broke Heart Blues, Black Water,* and *Because It Is Bitter,* and *Because It Is My Heart.* Her stories have appeared in publications as diverse as *Harper's Magazine, Playboy, Granta,* and the *Paris Review* and have been anthologized in *The O. Henry Awards, The Pushcart Prize, The Best American Short Stories of the Century,* and *The Best American Mystery Stories of the Century.* A recipient of the National Book Award for her novel *Them* and the PEN/Malamud Award for Achievement in the Short Story, Oates has been a member since 1978 of the American Academy of Arts and Letters and is the Roger S. Berlind Distinguished Professor of the Humanities at Princeton University.

ALICE ELLIOTT DARK is the author of a novel, *Think of England,* and two collections of short stories, *In the Gloaming* and *Naked to the Waist.* Her work has appeared in the *New Yorker, Harper's, Redbook, Double Take, Prize Stories: The O. Henry Awards,*

*Best American Short Stories 1994,* and *Best American Short Stories of the Century.* "In the Gloaming," a story, was made into films by HBO and Trinity Playhouse. She lives in Montclair, New Jersey, with her husband and son.

ALBERT MOBILIO is a Whiting Writers' Award recipient, and he won the 1998 National Book Critics Circle Award for reviewing. His books of poetry include *Bendable Siege, The Geographics,* and *Me with Animal Towering.* He teaches writing at New York University.

More than two decades after founding *Ms.* magazine, GLORIA STEINEM remains America's most influential, eloquent, and revered feminist. Her 1992 book *Revolution from Within: A Book of Self-Esteem* was a number-one best-seller and has been translated into eleven languages. She continues to travel widely as a speaker and feminist organizer.

KATE MILLETT'S Columbia University dissertation, *Sexual Politics* (1970) placed her at the forefront of the women's movement. Her political works include *The Prostitution Papers* (1973) and *The Politics of Cruelty* (1994). Millett has also published works on a number of personal issues, including her autobiography, *Flying* (1974) and *Sita* (1977), which is the story of a doomed romantic relationship. Also a visual artist, Millett founded the Women's Art Colony Farm and has shown her work internationally.

CLARE BOOTHE LUCE (1903–1987) held editorial positions on such magazines as *Vogue* and *Vanity Fair* during the early 1930s. Her plays *The Women* (1936), *Kiss the Boys Goodbye* (1938), and *Margin for Error* (1939) were notable for their acid wit; all were later filmed. Luce, a Republican, represented Connecticut in the U.S. House of Representatives from 1943 to 1947 and was the United States ambassador to Italy from 1953 to 1957.

MARGE PIERCY is an acclaimed American novelist, essayist, and poet best known for fiction with a feminist slant. Her novels include *Women on the Edge; He, She and It; City of Darkness, City of Light; Storm Tide* (with Ira Wood); and *Three Women.* Her memoir, *Sleeping with Cats,* has just been published by Morrow/HarperCollins. Her books of poetry include *The Moon Is Always Female, Circles on the Water, What Are Big Girls Made Of?, Early Grrrl,* and *The Art of Blessing the Day.*

Feminist film writer and critic MOLLY HASKELL has written for numerous publications, including the *Village Voice, New York, Vogue, The New York Times Book Review, Mirabella, Esquire,* and *The Nation.* She has served as an artistic director of the Sarasota French Film Festival, and as associate professor of film at Barnard College and adjunct professor of film at Columbia University. Her books include *From Reverence to Rape: The Treatment of Women in the Movies,* her 1990 memoir, *Love and Other Infectious Diseases,* and a collection of essays and interviews called *Holding My Own in No Man's Land: Women and Men, Film and Feminists* (1997).

SABRINA BARTON has published articles on Hitchcock and on the woman's psychothriller. She is an Assistant Professor in the English Department at the University of Texas, Austin, where she teaches courses on film and gender.

LORE SEGAL is a novelist, translator, essayist, and writer of children's books. She has recently retired from teaching at Ohio State University and lives in New York. Her books include *Other People's Houses, Her First American, Tell Me a Mitzi, The Juniper Tree and Other Tales from Grimm.*

Academy Award- and Emmy-winning film and stage actor SIR LAURENCE OLIVIER (1907–1989) was best known for his roles in Shakespearean works. His films include *Pride and Prejudice* (1940), *Henry V* (1944) and *Hamlet* (1948). He headed London's National Theatre Company from 1962 to 1973, and England's premier theater awards are named in his honor.

CATHERINE TEXIER was born and raised in France and lives in New York City. She is the author of three novels: *Panic Blood, Love Me Tender,* and *Chloé l'Atlantique* (written in French, her native tongue), and a memoir, *Breakup* (Doubleday, 1998), which was translated into nine languages. She was coeditor, with Joel Rose, of the literary magazine *Between C and D,* and has coedited, with him, two anthologies of short fiction: *Between C and D* and *Love Is Strange.* She is the recipient of a National Endowment for the Arts Award and a New York Foundation for the Arts Fellowship. Her new novel, *Victorine,* is due out from Pantheon in 2003.

EVAN ZIMROTH'S novel *Gangsters* won the National Jewish Book Award in 1996. She is also the author of *Collusion: Memoir of a Young Girl and Her Ballet Master* (1999) and two collections of poetry: *Dead, Dinner, or Naked* (1993) and *Giselle Considers Her Future* (1997).

DENNIS GRUNES received his Ph.D. in English from the State University of New York at Buffalo in 1974. Essays of his have appeared in *Studies in the Humanities, Ball State University Forum, CLA Journal, Essays in Literature, American Transcendental Quarterly,* and *American Imago.*

LISA SHEA is the author of *Hula,* a novel reissued by W. W. Norton in the summer of 2001. She is at work on a second novel, *The Free World,* a book of nonfiction, and is the recipient of a

Whiting Writer's Award. She has taught creative writing at Barnard College, the University of Massachusetts at Amherst Graduate MFA Program, New York University, and the University of the South at Sewanee, Tennessee, where she was the Tennessee Williams Fellow. She works as a freelance journalist and lives in Brooklyn with her son Jonathan and their pet Yorkie, Scarlet.

MELISSA HOLBROOK PIERSON is the author of *The Perfect Vehicle* and *Dark Horses and Black Beauties.* She lives in upstate New York.

YONA ZELDIS MCDONOUGH'S articles and fiction have appeared in *The New York Times Magazine, Harper's Bazaar, Family Circle, Lilith, Cosmopolitan, Metropolitan Home, Redbook, Bride's,* and *Modern Bride.* She is the editor of *The Barbie Chronicles: A Living Doll Turns Forty* (Touchstone, 1999) as well as numerous books for children. Her first novel, *The Four Temperaments,* is being published by Doubleday in 2002.